8/75

THE ECONOMIC CAUSES OF WAR

THE ECONOMIC
CAUSES OF WAR

by

LIONEL ROBBINS

Professor of Economics in the
University of London

NEW YORK

Howard Fertig

1968

PRINTED IN THE UNITED STATES OF AMERICA
BY NOBLE OFFSET PRINTERS, INC.

ANALYTICAL TABLE OF CONTENTS

CONTENTS

To A. G. G.
with gratitude and affection

PREFACE TO THE 1968 EDITION

I GREATLY welcome the proposal for a reprint of this essay. Published in the early months of the Second World War, the first edition was soon exhausted and, in these conditions, the original publisher showing no disposition to reprint, it passed out of view and, so far as I am aware, has been noticed very little ever since. Yet of all my writings of the inter-war period, it is one of the few with which I now feel any considerable sense of identity. Re-reading it after twenty-five years, although I have found some things which today I would put a little differently, I have found little that I would wish to retract and much which I still believe needs to be said.

There are, however, two matters on which some additional comment seems to be called for.

The first relates to possible causes of war in the age in which we now live. It is, I think, clear that we have moved a long way from the period when, as described in these pages, the fear of possible exclusion from economic opportunities played a considerable part in diplomatic tension. Japanese aggression was perhaps a classic case of this type of causation. But as already noted in my text, the motives inspiring Hitler and the Nazis were of a different order and so infused with purely psychopathological material as largely to escape any classification as economic. And the shadows under which we live today, the tensions between East and West, are certainly ideological rather than economic in origin. When Mr. Krushchev caused to be placed on Cuba installations for the discharge of nuclear weapons, he was not thinking of a possible gain or loss of markets. The determination of the government of the United States to prevent the extension of communism is not based on fear of impoverishment.

Nevertheless, I venture to submit that the type of analysis here presented has still a place in the rational discussion of the possible causes of war. It fits very well the period of history in regard to which the Marxian theories here discussed were originally elaborated. And although conditions today make these theories even less plausible than they were then, yet they are still believed by many. Millions of people in the Soviet Union and elsewhere in Communist countries believe that the major wars of the modern age have been the result of the machinations of profit-seeking capitalists. The quotation from Mr. E. M. Forster in the first chapter of this essay is still characteristic of the attitude of many sensitive and intelligent persons in western countries who have not made an independent examination of the evidence. Moreover, although the danger of war in the present age springs chiefly from causes which are not to be described as economic, it is still true, or so it seems to me, that the powers of independent sovereign states to pursue economic and financial policies inimical to the prosperity of others are an important factor tending to international disunity and hence to situations which may be exploited by power politics actuated by non-economic motives.

This brings me to the second point on which I have to comment, which relates to conceptions of political reorganisations designed to minimize such frictions. The essay here reproduced ends with a section written in the first weeks of war, pleading passionately for the creation of a United States of Europe within which German creativeness and energy might serve the common weal rather than periodically disrupting it. It also contains a footnote referring to plans for a wider Atlantic Union put forward by Mr. Clarence Streit and others, in which I express cordial appreciation of the idea but considerable scepticism concerning its practicability. At that time, I did not conceive the possibility of an isolationist United States allowing itself once more to be involved in the internecine quarrels of Europe.

A great deal has happened since then. Japanese and Nazi aggression destroyed isolationism during the war; and since then, fortunately for the rest of us, the hostility of the Soviet Union and later of China — whether based on fear or on expansionist ambition we need not enquire — has prevented any serious recrudescence thereof. With its massive armaments and its incomparable economic power, the United States is today the active leader and defender of the civilisation of the West.

Such gigantic changes of circumstance could not but affect the perspective of thought regarding the possibilities of the future. In the years immediately following the end of the war, despairing of the stability and political reliability of some of the states of Western Europe and revolted by the anti-Americanism current among influential continental politicians and thinkers whose very existence had been saved by American intervention, I abandoned my earlier position and argued against British entry into a purely European Union, setting my hopes on a larger structure developing gradually from the North Atlantic Alliance. In this I now think I was wrong, not in my conviction of the fundamental necessity of preserving the link with the United States and Canada, but in my failure to realise the potentialities both of the creation, in these circumstances, of a United Western Europe and of the part which could be played in it by Great Britain. I underestimated the inability of those responsible for British policy to see where their true interest lay — in a vigorous development of something like Atlantic Union — and I failed to foresee the colossal folly of the Suez episode which deprived us of our standing as a first-class power with freedom to take influential initiatives. At the present time, therefore, I once more support an approach to the more limited union with Western Europe. So I am back in a frame of mind in which the peroration of this essay is not something which I wish to repudiate.

But after all that has happened, and having regard to the perilous equilibrium of the world, I must emphasize that I continue to regard the more limited association as a *pis aller*, a preliminary, perhaps an inescapable preliminary, to a more perfect and larger union later on; and I remain intensely apprehensive of the powerful currents of opinion on this side of the water which depict United Europe, not as a stage in the evolution of something wider, but as the creation of an independent "third force" upholding values which, on this view, the descendants of Benjamin Franklin and Abraham Lincoln are unable to understand. This is a conception which I find intellectually unacceptable and morally antipathetic: an ignoble ideology of the second rate coffeehouse, without vision or common sense, an apt index of the spiritual myopia of those who preach it — or are taken in by it.

Robbins

The London School of Economics
October 1967

8

PREFACE

THE following essay is based upon five lectures which I was privileged to deliver, in the spring of this year, at the *Institut Universitaire de Hautes Études Internationales* of Geneva. I have completely rewritten my manuscript and considerably extended the treatment of certain aspects of my subject. But the substance and, with one exception noted below, the general scheme of arrangement remain the same. I should like to take this opportunity of once more thanking M. Rappard and his colleagues for their invitation and for the indulgence with which they listened to my story. How much of all that was most stimulating and inspiring in the period between two wars is typified in their lovely college by the lake. Long may it flourish, an oasis of sanity in a mad world, to preserve and advance the great principles of international citizenship for which it so conspicuously stands.

In deciding to publish at this stage, I have had many hesitations. I do not think that even the most hostile critic can mistake the pretentions of my slender essay for those of a full-blown treatise. But there are sections where I am conscious that, even on this plane, further elaboration would have been desirable; and there are certain features which I contemplated in my original plan, which do not appear at all, notably appendices on the detailed history of the controversies concerning the Marxian theory of imperialism and on the rise of neo-mercantilism in Germany. But circumstances have not been favourable. Ever since I commenced to work in this field, I have never sat down to work without wondering if war would come before my projects were completed. And now, confronted with the alternatives of publishing something less than I had intended or of postponing publication perhaps indefinitely, I have had reluctantly to choose the former. I will not conceal my belief that my conclusions, which, of course, are not exclusively my own but rather the development of a great number of converging lines of investigation,[1] are of considerable relevance to the solution of the problems which we now face; and I would rather present a target to academic critics than leave unsaid the least thing which might conceivably be helpful.

The main body of the essay is an attempt to get into proper perspective the part played by economic motives and economic institutions in the causation of modern war. I hope that this will be useful in itself, for it deals with a subject about which there has recently been much confusion. But, from my point of view at least, much more important is the demonstration, for which all the earlier argument is a preparation, of the fundamental inappropriateness to modern conditions of the present political organization of the world and the necessity of replacing the independent sovereign states by larger federal unions. I first developed this view, some four years ago, in a course of lectures, also delivered at Geneva, which were subsequently incorporated in my *Economic Planning and International Order*; and the publication since then of works by Mr. Lionel Curtis and Mr. Clarence Streit, which, approaching the general problem of international relations from starting-points very different from mine, reach substantially the same solution, encourages me to believe that the conclusions I then put forward were substantially on the right lines. I have not repeated in this essay the

---

[1] I would like to pay special tribute to the historical researches of Professor Jacob Viner and his school, especially Mr. Staley, without which much of chap. iii could never have been written.

systematic arguments of the earlier book where I tried to show that, starting, as it were, with a blank sheet, and trying to reason out from general principles the requirements of a sensible world order, one arrived necessarily at the idea of federation. But I believe that an examination of the causes which have actually led to war in the past and which will certainly do so again and again in the future if action is not taken, leads irresistibly to the same conclusion; and I hope that the analysis and the historical examples here provided will do something to drive it home. In the last section, I have ventured to speculate a little concerning possible developments in Europe; I hope that, at this point, the relevance of the whole argument to our present situation will be readily apparent. The ordeals through which we are passing are surely one tremendous object lesson of the truth of the theme that we must federate or perish. I do not know anything for which men would fight more willingly than the idea of a Europe from which the danger of recurrent civil war was banished, and I know no way by which this can be achieved save by some form of federation.

In the course of lectures upon which this essay has been based, following long established academic tradition, the first section was devoted to questions of definition and procedure. I do not think that it inflicted undue pain upon my hearers, nor do I think that it is likely in itself to present any special difficulties to laymen. But the plane of discussion is much more abstract than that of the rest; and for this reason, in preparing a version which aspires to be not merely intelligible but even interesting to the general reader, I have placed it at the end as an appendix. I hope that this will not prevent professional economists, at least, from glancing through it. The investigation of the meaning of an economic cause which is its main content does something, I think, to round off the discussions of the nature of the economic, in which some of us have participated recently.

I have to express my gratitude to various friends who have helped me at different stages. In particular I should mention Professor Hayek, who is responsible for a great improvement of arrangement, and Mr. L. G. Robinson, who advised me on certain matters of diplomatic history. Mr. Robinson must be exonerated from all blame for my amateurish blunderings. But he has at least this general responsibility in that it was at his lectures many years ago that I first came to love puzzling about this intricate subject and the fascinating problems it involves.

Lionel Robbins

The London School of Economics
September 16*th*, 1939

THE ECONOMIC CAUSES OF WAR

CHAPTER I

INTRODUCTION

1 *The Menace of Modern War*

HUMAN life to-day is darkened by a dreadful shadow — the shadow of international war. In many parts of the world, war has actually broken out; in others, preparation for war is the mainspring of daily activity. At work, in our homes, in public places, the reverberations are inescapable. Never in history have the thoughts of so many human beings been dominated by this continuous fear.

This state of affairs is inimical to our type of civilization — if not throughout the world as a whole, at any rate in the continent of Europe. Whatever may have been its influence in the past, whether or not it ever had a civilizing function, to-day the nature of war is such that the very possibility of its occurrence is incompatible with the persistence of what has been called the Great Society. If war breaks out, it brings chaos and destruction. If peace is maintained but the danger of war persists, the measures of preparation which modern technique makes necessary, must gradually absorb the whole energies of the nations; wealth must diminish, civil liberty be limited, the arts decay and the natural sciences, which should be the liberators of humanity, be devoted almost wholly to its destruction. We must remove this danger or we must eventually revert to simpler forms of society.

But to do this we must remove the underlying conditions which make war possible. It is not enough to bring about a temporary alleviation of the tension by military victory and by power groupings of the traditional kind, essential as that may be at the moment. For, as we know to our cost, military victory by itself settles nothing permanently; and power groupings are inherently unstable. If there are underlying conditions conducive to conflict, then, sooner or later, conflict will emerge. After the great struggle of 1914-18 was over, it was thought that there would be no more war in our generation. But to-day war has once more broken out and the jibes of those who urged that war was to be regarded as a permanent feature of human society appear to be justified. For those who believe that there is still hope of improvement in more knowledge of the working of human institutions, there can be no more urgent task than the discovery of the ultimate causes of war.

2 *The Object of the Essay*

It is the aim of these chapters to attempt to contribute to this solution. But the problem will be approached from a special point of view. They will not begin by inquiring concerning the causes of war in general, though that is a problem upon which it is hoped eventually to throw some light. They will begin rather by inquiring to what extent war can be regarded as being due to economic causes — either particular types of economic motives or particular types of institutional settings amid which such motives may be conceived to be engendered. This will inevitably involve some discussion of the part played by non-economic factors; for there is no desire to claim an exclusive status for economic causes. And, before the end is reached, it will be found necessary to inquire concerning certain wider political and sociological questions. But the main structure of the argument, if not its ultimate focus of reference, will be concerned with economic causes.

Two considerations have dictated this mode of procedure.

In the first place, it seems reasonable to suppose that inquiry on these lines may be fruitful. Economic factors underlie so many of the happenings of social life, that it is plausible to assume that here too they may be found to be operative. It would be very surprising if we were to find that there were no economic factors involved in the causation of any wars. An inquiry which commences from the economic aspect therefore has some prospect of starting at least on firm earth.

But, beyond this, there is another reason which perhaps has weighed even more in determining the form of the present investigation. At the present time it is widely believed that the occurrence of war in our own times is exclusively, or at least predominantly, due to a special kind of economic cause. It is thought that the institutions of private property and the market, in their present stage of development, tend inevitably to breed international conflict — that war is a necessary by-product of the capitalist system. This belief is held, not merely by the adherents of a particular political creed but by many of the most disinterested and sensitive spirits of our day. 'Bourgeois born and in my fifties', writes Mr. E. M. Forster, 'I feel that communism will submerge all the things I have learnt to love. But I am deeply impressed by the communist argument which ascribes war to the capitalist system and I feel that the hysteria which prevents people from examining this argument ... is most discreditable.'[1]

It is impossible to exaggerate the importance of this contention. If it is true, then the main duty of our generation is to sweep away the institutions which give rise to this horror. If it is false, it may lead to a misdirection of effort

[1] *Time and Tide*, November 23rd, 1935.

which divides the forces of goodwill and diverts attention from the real causes of conflict. Surely it deserves the most scrupulous attention by all who have any competence in these matters. That at least has been the conviction which originally gave rise to this study and which has dictated the form in which it is cast.

3 *The Plan of Inquiry*

The plan of the essay is very simple. It will begin with an exposition of the main outlines of the relevant Marxian theories, in particular the theory of imperialism which receives its classical exposition in the work of Lenin. It will then go on to test this theory in the light of history. The result of this test being largely negative, an attempt will then be made to formulate an explanation of the economic causes of war at once more comprehensive in scope and more in correspondence with the facts. Finally inquiry will be made into the political and social setting in which the causes diagnosed are likely to be operative. The appendix explains certain matters of definition and procedure which have been assumed throughout the main argument.

CHAPTER II

THE MARXIAN THEORY OF IMPERIALISM

1 *The Economic Interpretation of War*

BELIEF that war may be due to economic causes is not of modern origin. The desire for gain has so often played a role in the generation of group conflict that it would be remarkable if its operation in this respect had not frequently been recognized. In fact, of course, this has often happened. From very early times historians have explained particular wars in terms of an economic motive; and, when the causes of war in general have come under discussion, the desire for wealth and material betterment has received at least its due share of recognition. It is indeed arguable that many of the confusions relating to the economic causes of war in modern times derive from the naive application to present-day conditions of modes of explanation chiefly applicable to conditions of the past. But whether this is so or not, the belief that it is only in our own times that we have begun to perceive the working of the economic factor can only rest upon ignorance. The idea that thinkers of earlier epochs explained wars only in terms of disputes involving religion, love, honour and lust for power and suchlike categories, and that it was left to the sophisticated minds of our own age to understand the importance of economic motives, may be fashionable but it is false.[1]

Nevertheless, there is a difference between earlier and

---

[1] In Book II of the *Republic*, for instance, Plato gives an explanation of the origins of war which is couched entirely in terms of economic causes.

more recent thought on these matters — a difference both of degree of generality and type of explanation. The older writers on these topics were content to explain particular wars in terms of particular economic causes or, if they were attempting to discuss the causes of war in general, to indicate various types of desire for gain as one of the possible causes and to leave it at that. It is the characteristic of more recent thought that it attempts to go beyond this — to describe the economic motive with greater technical precision and to explain its operation in terms of wider generalizations relating to the whole structure of society. Its explanations are not merely incidental or classificatory, they are analytical and systematic. Whether great success has as yet attended these efforts is perhaps an open question. But that they do constitute an endeavour to achieve a wider kind of knowledge is undeniable. They are a part of the effort of the last two hundred years to achieve, in regard to the phenomena of society, a body of systematic knowledge, comparable in its generality with the propositions of the natural sciences.

Of such attempts by far the most ambitious and the most influential is the so-called Marxian theory which attributes the occurrence of war in recent times to the existence of capitalist institutions of a certain stage of development. Although, as we shall see shortly, it has a certain restriction of application in time, it is more comprehensive in its claims, more far reaching in its implications than any other theory relating to these matters; and it has had an influence far transcending the sphere of communist propaganda in any narrow sense. It has affected our interpretation of the past and our hopes and fears concerning the future. It has affected the course of politics; and it has even influenced — not perhaps with very felicitous results — the writing of poetry. It would be difficult to overestimate the extent to which, in our war-darkened days, it has dominated the thoughts of large numbers of people.

For this reason, and because the testing out of a definite hypothesis is a good way of getting some order into our perceptions of a complicated body of material, it will be convenient to approach the main subject by analysing the grounds on which this theory has been supported and by attempting to test it by reference to facts.

2 *General Characteristics of the Marxian Theory*

There are two general characteristics of the Marxian theory which it is desirable to recognize before proceeding to any detail.

In the first place, it is a theory with an explicit historical limitation. It may be that the more general propositions of the Marxian philosophy imply that all wars are due to economic causes; certainly some versions of the materialist interpretation of history would seem to justify that view. But the theory to be examined here, the theory of imperialism, makes no such universal claim. It professes only to interpret a particular phase of history, the period of fully developed capitalism. Only the wars of this epoch are explained in terms of this particular economic cause.

It follows, therefore, that it can only be examined within these terms of reference. It is no use attempting to refute the Marxian theory of imperialism by reference to cases of war occurring in other historical periods — 'genuine' crusades, blood feuds among primitive peoples, quarrels of prestige under feudalism and so on. Whether it is right or wrong, it refers only to the wars of the capitalist epoch.

But — and this is the second general characteristic to which it is necessary to draw attention — within this epoch its claims are comprehensive. It does urge that, within this period, all wars and international friction, or at any rate all important wars and all important frictions, are due to the existence of the capitalist form of society. It is not merely a claim that sometimes the influence of particular groups of capitalists may have led to war or the danger of war; it claims, rather, that always the underlying cause has been the existence of capitalism. It is, therefore, not merely an historical explanation of particular wars, but a general explanation of the consequences of a certain form of social organization. There will be occasion later on to cite full evidence of this claim. But it is important that from the outset its nature should be clearly recognized. For obviously there is all the difference in the world between a theory which holds that certain groups of property owners may exercise a sinister influence sometimes and a theory which holds that it is inevitable that they should do so all the time.

3 *The Underconsumption Theory*

What then are the grounds by which this theory is supported?

If regard is paid to the confidence with which its claims are asserted and the pivotal position which it occupies in the strategy of communist propaganda,[1] it might reason-

---

[1] It is perhaps worth noting how pivotal it is. It is a fundamental claim of the Marxian position that under capitalism, the condition of the majority of the people is bound to deteriorate. Up to the outbreak of the Great War of 1914-18, this seemed to be in obvious contradiction to the facts; and even since then, in those parts of the world not immediately affected by the post-war chaos, the improvement of real incomes has continued. So that it would seem to be a legitimate objection to the Marxian theory to argue that any deterioration that has taken place is chiefly to be attributed to this factor rather than to the inevitable tendencies of the dynamics of capitalist society. If, however, the Great War itself can be shown to be the inevitable result of the capitalist system, the apparent contradiction disappears and the 'theory of increasing misery' is vindicated.

ably be expected that the main outlines of its analytical and historical justification would be a matter of common agreement among writers of this school, as easily accessible as the main outlines, let us say, of the labour theory of value. And there can be little doubt that the general public which discusses these matters, not to mention the many 'bourgeois' historians who profess to have been influenced by Marxian theory, have assumed this to be the case. I myself am certainly willing to confess that, until some years ago when I began to take a special interest in these matters and to seek out the original texts, I was definitely under this impression. The Marxian theory of imperialism, I thought, rested upon a somewhat rigid form of the underconsumption theory of the trade cycle. Because there was chronic tendency for the working classes to have too little to spend, there developed a struggle for international markets which tended from time to time to culminate in war. That, I thought — and, I am sorry to say, occasionally even taught — was *the* Marxian theory of imperialism. But in fact this is not so. The theory of imperialism, or the theory of catastrophe (*Zusammenbruch*), as it is sometimes called, is not a matter on which there is general agreement among Marxian writers. There is no clear guidance from Marx; and, as anyone who will take the trouble to consult easily accessible literature can find out for himself, among the followers of Marx, there is the sharpest possible dissension. They agree, of course, that it is capitalism which is the culprit. But on the question why it is the culprit, such undeniable communists as, for instance, Rosa Luxemburg and Lenin, take radically different views and dispute among themselves with all the vigour of economists not attached to any particular party creed. They become, as it were, human beings like the rest of us, liable alike to error and occasional intellectual

23

progress. Even if we discount all minor expository differences, it must be recognized that there are at least two communist theories of the economic causes of war; and any survey of this question, which is to do anything like justice to the subject, must take some account of each and weigh their respective claims to be 'orthodox'.[1]

We may commence with those theories which stress the alleged chronic deficiency of markets. Their origin is earlier in time; and much more than the later, and perhaps more 'orthodox', rival views, they form the basis of what is popularly believed to be Marxian teaching on this matter.

The general background of these theories is provided by the underconsumption theories of Malthus and Sismondi. Sismondi in particular throws out hints which may well have furnished the basis for more systematic thought on this matter. In his *Nouveaux Principes d'Économie Politique*[2] he asserts that 'By the concentration of fortunes . . . the internal market is continually narrowing and, more and more, industry is reduced to discovering foreign markets'. Here clearly enough is the main theme of this form of the theory we are examining.

But Sismondi was not a systematic writer. Moreover, perhaps, he was much too much of an historian to wish to make an observation of this sort the basis of any very comprehensive theory regarding historical development. Much more important in this respect is the German economist, Rodbertus, who, in a pamphlet of 1858,[3]

---

[1] The account which follows is necessarily very limited. No attempt has been made to provide an exhaustive survey of the history of such theories — a task which would very well repay further research. An excellent summary is provided by E. M. WINSLOW, *Marxian, Liberal and Sociological Theories of Imperialism*, 'Journal of Political Economy', XXXIX, December 1931, pp. 713-18.

[2] 2nd edition, 1927, p. 361.

[3] *Die Handelskrisen und die Hypothekennoth der Grundbesitzer.*

develops a theory of the tendencies of capitalist development which sets the tone of most of what has been written
on this subject ever since.

It would be a mistake, he urges, to regard the crisis
which was then raging as being in any way due to lack of
money. (Such repudiations of any appeal to monetary
causes have been a leading feature of underconsumption
theories until very recently.) The cause is, not lack of
money, but a wrong distribution of income which brings
it about that too much is invested, too little spent on consumption. This maldistribution is no transitory phenomenon; it is an organic disease of modern society springing
essentially from the nature of the property system. It
follows, therefore, that all the so-called remedies are merely
palliatives. 'All that can be done to guard against future
outbreaks is only the double-edged weapon of an enlargement of the foreign market. The present struggles to do
this spring from this fundamental disease. Because productivity continually rises in the home market and the
purchasing power of the people remains the same, trade
must find an outlet in external markets . . . Every new
market thus found means a suspension of the central social
problem. Colonization has the same effect . . . But, because the world is limited, the acquisition of new markets
must one day cease . . . Then the social question will have
to be solved.'

Here, although without specific mention of the probability of war, we have all the essentials of the underconsumptionist form of the theory of imperialism. Explicit
connection of the struggle for markets with diplomatic
friction and war is the work of more recent writers. Of
these we may take as representative the work of Rosa
Luxemburg in Germany and of Mr. J. A. Hobson in
England.

Rosa Luxemburg's *Akkumulation des Kapitals* is probably the most uncompromising statement of the underconsumption theory ever put forward by an intelligent person. All saving under capitalistic conditions tends to produce stagnation and depression. Even the schemata of Volume II of *Das Kapital* in which Marx tries to show how, at different stages of accumulation, the process of capitalist circulation proceeds, fail to show how the product can be sold at a profit if accumulation is actually taking place. The Marxian theory of capital in the technical sense of the term was greatly superior, she argues, to that of the classical economists.[1] But it is essentially static in character. It fails to show how, under dynamic conditions, surplus value can actually be realized. And in fact, she goes on to argue, under strictly capitalistic conditions the problem is actually insoluble. Under strictly capitalistic conditions, there is no one to buy those products which the capitalists wish ultimately to realize as surplus value. In order that the system may function at all there must be a buyer outside — a *third person*, to use the phrase which the Luxemburg analysis has made famous. There must be a non-capitalistic world side by side with the capitalistic.

[1] There is indeed much to be said for the view that, in this part of his work, Marx did perceive problems which tended to be concealed by the Smithian formula that the price of the product can be resolved into wages, profits and rent. It is doubtful whether, in spite of Mr. Dobb's ingenious apologia, at the present day, there is anything much to be saved from the wreckage of the labour theory of value of *Das Kapital*: the verdict of economists since Jevons on this point seems in need of no very drastic revision. But while we know how to put the theory of capital much more clearly and elegantly than did Marx, it is only fair to say that, in this respect, in many points he was considerably ahead of his time. Few economists to-day seem to find time to read on into Volume II — which, considering the limited duration of human life, is perhaps not extraordinary. But if they did, they would find that, on this point at least, Marx seems to forget Hegel and propaganda and, like the good classical economist he sometimes was, to become absorbed in the study of a purely intellectual problem.

It is not difficult to see how such an analysis may be made the basis for a fully developed theory of imperialism; and this indeed is the culmination of Luxemburg's argument. The third person, the non-capitalistic *deus ex machina*, may be found in the natural economy at home; hence, in the early stages of capitalism, the continual pressure to break up the self-sufficient agricultural communities at home. But it may be found, too, overseas; hence the urge of the capitalist powers to appropriate the non-capitalist parts of the world outside Europe and North America — the Chinese wars, the scramble for Africa, the ever-increasing pressure of imperialist aggression. Hence, too, the inevitable collision of these powers as the area of non-capitalist economy still to be exploited becomes narrower and narrower. With relentless eloquence the author describes the increasing tribulations which must lead to the final catastrophe.

Mr. Hobson's view is not radically dissimilar from this, although, as might be expected, it is stated with much more subtlety and reservation and, as we shall see, the underlying theoretical analysis is perhaps capable of a more favourable interpretation. The fullest statement of his views is to be found in his *Imperialism*, a work whose immediate occasion was the controversy aroused by the Boer War, but which represents a logical extension of general underconsumptionist views developed much earlier. His argument can be best stated in his own words.[1]

'Everywhere', he says, 'appear excessive powers of production, excessive capital in search of investment. It is admitted by all business men that the growth of the powers of production in their own country exceeds the growth in consumption, that more goods can be produced than can

---

[1] I have selected salient passages from pp. 80-8.

be sold at a profit and that more capital exists than can find remunerative investment.

'It is this economic condition of affairs that forms the taproot of imperialism. If the consuming public in this country raised its standard of consumption to keep pace with every rise of productive powers, there would be no excess of goods or capital clamorous to use imperialism in order to find markets: foreign trade would indeed exist but there would be no difficulty in exchanging a small surplus of our manufactures for the food and raw material we annually absorbed and all the savings that we made could find employment, if we chose, in home industry.

'If the apportionment of income were such as to evoke no excessive saving, full constant employment for capital and labour would be furnished at home... The struggle for markets, the greater eagerness of producers to sell than of consumers to buy is the crowning proof of a false economy of distribution.'

Mr. Hobson's influence has far transcended that of any other writer on these subjects, save perhaps Lenin. It is probably from him rather than from the orthodox communists, that the majority of lesser writers, economic historians and general political journalists have, directly or indirectly, absorbed the view that it is capitalism which in our time is responsible for international war. Whether this drastic conclusion is indeed to be drawn from Mr. Hobson's own reserved and qualified statements is perhaps an open question. But of the importance of his work in the formation of the intellectual atmosphere of our time there can be no doubt.

4 *The Logical Significance of the Underconsumption Theory*
It will be useful, before proceeding further, to pause for a moment to inquire a little into the analytical validity

of the views we have so far examined and to attempt to assess their significance in regard to the central proposition which they are supposed to support. To what extent is the under-consumption theory analytically consistent and what support does it furnish for the view that it is capitalism which is responsible for war?

There can be little doubt that, in the form in which it was stated by Rosa Luxemburg, the theory is inadmissible. There is no schematic difficulty in depicting the creation of real capital; Marx was right here and Rosa Luxemburg was creating imaginary difficulties. Of course, in the process of capital creation, the rate of return may fall and, as we shall see when we come to examine the views of Lenin and his followers, it is quite possible to build on this a logically consistent hypothesis regarding imperialist expansion.[1] But it is not correct to argue that the creation of real capital in itself produces a situation in which the final product cannot be disposed of within the closed circle of the capitalist system. A God in the machine from outside is not necessary.

Much the same strictures must apply to all those forms of the underconsumption theory — and this certainly includes some, though perhaps not all, versions of Mr. Hobson's theory — which rely upon the assumption that too much is actually *invested*. Investment is a cost-reducing process and, provided that prices are allowed to fall sufficiently, then, even with constant money incomes, there is no reason why the product of increased real investment should not be fully disposed of. All the examples which purport to prove the contrary are worked out on the assumption of constant prices and constant incomes. But this misconceives the problem. There is nothing in

---

[1] It should be noted that the word hypothesis is used here. We are not yet discussing the consistency of hypotheses with the facts.

general economic theory which justifies the belief that until the rate of return drops to zero, the product of properly directed investment cannot be disposed of at a profit.

In recent years, however, attempts have been made to justify the general underconsumptionist outlook in terms, not of excessive investment, but of a disposition to make savings which do not succeed in finding their way into investment. If the propensity to save is high and if the disposition to hold cash or cash balances is such as, with a given quantity of money, to maintain interest rates higher than the general rate of return over cost, then, by a curtailment of money income usually accompanied by unemployment and depression, the amount which is actually saved is forcibly restricted to the amount actually invested. Given the quantity of money — this is a fundamental assumption — and the other independent variables, it is possible, as Dr. Oskar Lange has shown,[1] to speak of an optimum propensity to consume; and if this is not reached, then under-employment and depression may result. It is very difficult to believe that anything of this sort has been in the minds of the majority of the exponents of underconsumption theories. Certainly it is quite foreign to the way of thinking of all those who have propounded theories of the kind of which that of Rosa Luxemburg is typical. But it is arguable that it is what some at least were fumbling after. In the case of Mr. Hobson, for instance, although he has usually developed his argument in terms of excessive investment, yet from time to time, in replying to criticism, he has made sundry references to the stickiness of interest rates, which perhaps entitle us to assume that something similar to the Keynesian analysis was also sometimes in his mind.

[1] *The Rate of Interest and the Optimum Propensity to Consume*, 'Economica', 1938, pp. 12-32.

Now there is nothing about this form of the theory which is analytically inconsistent. It represents a state of affairs which certainly might exist in the world of reality. It suffers from no fault of internal construction. It does not present those obvious targets to logical markmanship which are the characteristics of earlier versions. Whether it is a state of affairs which is generally prevalent — whether, as Mr. Keynes and his followers seem to think, it provides *the* explanation of the trade cycle, or whether, as is the view of those who adopt a more eclectic attitude, it only describes an explanation of *possible* turning points and of a restricted phase of depressions which may have been brought about by other causes — these are matters of acute controversy upon which the verdict of empirical investigation is still ambiguous.

Fortunately, for the purposes of this chapter, it is not necessary to solve these unsettled questions. Whether the theory is right or wrong, whether it fits the facts of the majority of depressions or whether it describes only certain exceptional cases, it does not prove the main contention of the Marxian case that the crisis is due to capitalism. For, as is obvious from Dr. Lange's exposition, this form of the underconsumption theory involves appeal to essentially monetary considerations. The deficiency it indicates is not a structural deficiency of the system of private property and free markets. It is a deficiency of the machinery for supplying money. For if, with a given quantity of money, the general demand for cash holdings is such that the proportion of saving which is attempted is beyond the optimum, then the injection of an additional supply of money would put things right again. In practice this may be an extraordinarily difficult thing to bring about. The general stickiness of the organization of financial markets may present most formidable obstacles. But the disease, if it exists, is a disease of the financial system, not a disease inseparable from the existence of capitalism. It is perhaps no accident that Mr. Keynes, who must be regarded as the leading exponent in our own day of this form of under-consumption theory, far from thinking that the remedies he proposes would abolish capitalism, has even claimed that they are the means of making capitalism both work-able and morally acceptable. There will be something more to be said about the struggle for markets and its various causes later on.[1] But at this stage of the argument we need not pursue this form of the theory any further.

5 *The Leninist Theory of Imperialism*

This does not mean, however, that we have disposed of the communist explanation of imperialism. It is doubtful whether the main stream of Marxian theory has ever been underconsumptionist in character. Certainly Rosa Luxem-burg was not accepted as orthodox. She was attacked most furiously on this point by Otto Bauer[2] and Bukharin;[3] and her whole theory has more recently been subjected to an exhaustive analysis by Grossmann who purports to show that, both deductively and inductively, it is false and misleading.[4] To discover the main grounds of the communist theory, as it is held at the present day, we must look to another group of writers.

The attitude of Marx to the whole question of imperial-ism is a matter of some ambiguity. In his main theoretical structure, he abstracted deliberately from considerations of foreign trade. The celebrated chapter on Colonies in Volume I of *Das Kapital* is designed simply to illustrate his

---

[1] See chaps. iv and v below.
[2] *Neue Zeit.*, 1913, Nr. 24.
[3] *Der Imperialismus und die Akkumulation des Kapitals*, Berlin, 1926.
[4] *Das Akkumulations – und Zuzammenbruchsgesetz des kapitalistischen Systems*, Leipzig, 1929.

general thesis regarding the exploitation of labour. There are *obiter dicta* on the causes of depression which were said by Rosa Luxemburg (who not unnaturally claimed to be the true interpreter of the master) to support her theory. But there seems little doubt that Marx's main theory of the trade cycle relied, not on the motive of under-consumption in the mode of Malthus and Sismondi, but rather upon the motive of disproportionality in the mode of Wilson and Spiethoff; and there is a passage in Volume II where he definitely goes out of his way to repudiate any suggestion that it is a deficiency of consumers' purchasing power which is the root of the difficulty.

'It is purely a tautology', he says, 'to say that crises are caused by the scarcity of solvent consumers or of a paying consumption. The capitalist system does not know any other mode of consumption but a paying one, except that of the pauper or of the "thief". If any commodities are unsaleable, it means that no solvent purchasers have been found for them, in other words consumers . . . But if one were to attempt to clothe this tautology with a semblance of a profounder justification by saying that the working class receive too small a portion of their own product and that the evil would be remedied by giving them a larger share of it or raising their wages, we should reply that crises are always preceded by a period in which wages rise generally and the working classes actually get a larger share of the annual product expected for consumption. From the point of view of "simple" (!) common sense, such a period should rather remove a crisis.'[1]

Engels adds the grim footnote: 'Advocates of the theory of crisis of Rodbertus are requested to make a note of this.'

At the present day it would be generally admitted by

[1] *Capital*, vol. II, pp. 475-6.

members of the Communist Party, that the orthodox communist theory is to be found in Lenin's monograph on imperialism.[1] It is this work which is held to contain the real explanation of the origins of the Great War and the necessary tendency to catastrophe of a world of capitalist states; and it is the theory underlying this analysis which must be set out and examined if we are to do justice to the main stream of communist thought on these matters.

It is necessary to note, at the outset of our inquiry, that Lenin's work does not depend at all upon the constructions of the underconsumption theory. Lenin quotes Mr. Hobson and praises his candour; and this has given rise to the view that his own contribution follows the same tradition. But this is not so. He quotes Mr. Hobson's facts rather than his theory. The main theoretical influence on Lenin is undoubtedly Hilferding's *Finanzkapital*; and, in this work the underconsumption theory is definitely rejected.

The central assumption of Lenin's theory is not underconsumption but the influence of monopoly finance and the struggle of capitalists to avert the secular tendency to a falling rate of profit.

As capitalism develops, he argues, the organization of production tends more and more to fall into the hands of monopolies. (Lenin quotes voluminous statistics to prove that this actually happens and assumes throughout that it is a technically inevitable development.) As these monopolies develop, they come more and more to control the governments of the various states; and 'national' policy is essentially the product of their influence. It is sound Marxian orthodoxy to assume that the state is necessarily the organ of the predominant type of economic

[1] *Imperialism, the Highest Stage of Capitalism.* Selected Works of V. I. Lenin, vol. v. An admirable gloss on the somewhat repellent exposition of Lenin is to be found in Dr. Maurice Dobb's essay on Imperialism in his *Political Economy and Capitalism.*

organization; and it is assumed throughout Lenin's book that the state in the period of *spätkapitalismus* is necessarily to be regarded as the instrument of monopolist strategy.

The operation of these monopolies, he goes on, is not confined to the area of the state in which they originate. Because of the economic interdependence of different areas, their interests extend far beyond the frontiers. And because there are many monopolies and many states these interests are often in conflict. This conflict is apparent in regard to raw materials. If monopoly profit is to be secure it must be immune from the control by other monopolies of essential raw material supplies. The great monopolies of the world are ceaselessly intriguing to secure for themselves, via the extension of the jurisdiction of the states they control, command over raw materials such as iron ore and oil; and Lenin thinks that part at least of the imperialist struggle is to be interpreted in this way.

But the main conflict is in the sphere of finance. Modern imperialism is essentially the clash of financial interests. The struggle for extensions of territory, for spheres of influence, and so on, is the struggle of rival groups of 'finance capital' seeking to extend their monopolies.

It is at this point that it is necessary to realize the influence on Lenin of the work of Rudolf Hilferding. To the English-speaking reader, be he liberal or socialist in outlook, there is something odd about the peculiar status attributed to the entity called 'finance capital'. Finance he can understand. Monopoly he can understand. In spite of the vagaries of professional economists, he has some conception of what is meant by the term capital in various contexts. But the extraordinary status accorded to 'finance capital' and the special literature devoted to this entity by certain continental writers is more than a little bewildering.

The solution is to be found in the special development of

the structure of German banking. As is well known, for many years before the War, the great German banks participated in the actual conduct of industrial enterprise to a much greater extent than anywhere else in the world. Their financial power was used more and more in carrying through the great mergers and consolidations so characteristic of German industrial development; and Central European Marxists, of whom Hilferding was an outstanding leader, regarded this development, not merely as constituting a special phase of the development of German institutions, but as a special stage of the development of capitalistic institutions in general — a model to which eventually all banking development would conform. Unless this is realized, the special significance which he, and following him Lenin, attached to this technical phrase, is apt to escape notice.

Whether Lenin was actually conscious of the extent to which the phenomena of finance capital in this peculiar sense were restricted to certain European countries is not clear. It might, perhaps, be argued that he believed that, although the direct connection between finance and monopolistic industry was less obvious elsewhere, yet nevertheless such a connection existed and might be treated as coming under the same general categories. At any rate, there can be no doubt that it is to the operations of high finance, struggling desperately to escape from the falling rate of profit which resulted from the development of domestic industry, that he attributed the main clashes of modern imperialism. 'The necessity for exporting capital arises from the fact that in the main centres, capitalism has become "over-ripe" and . . . capital cannot find profitable investment.'[1] 'The characteristic feature of imperialism is *not* industrial capital *but* finance capital.'[2]

[1] Op. cit., p. 57.   [2] Ibid., p. 83.

36

Lenin actually gives a list of five 'essential features' of the imperialist stage of capitalist development; and if we are to do justice to his theory, it is perhaps as well that we should set them out in his own terms. The five features are as follows: the prose style is that of Lenin's translator.

(1) 'The concentration of production and capital developed to such a stage that it creates monopolies which play a decisive role in economic life.'

(2) 'The merging of bank capital with industrial capital on the basis of "finance capital" of a financial oligarchy.'

(3) 'The export of capital which has become extremely important as distinguished from the export of commodities.

(4) 'The formation of international capitalist monopolies which share the world among themselves.'

(5) 'The territorial division of the whole world among the greatest capitalist powers is completed.'[1]

Once this stage has arrived, he urges, clashes of interest and war are inevitable.

This, in short, is the positive part of his theory. But in order that there may be no mistaking his attitude, Lenin makes critical comment upon certain alternative views from which he wishes to dissociate himself.

Thus he declaims against those who had urged that the characteristic of imperialism is agrarian annexation. On the contrary he urges, 'The characteristic feature of imperialism is that it strives to annex not only agricultural but even highly industrialized regions. (German appetite for Belgium, French appetite for Lorraine.)'[2] He thus dissociates himself completely from the attitude of Rosa Luxemburg. No 'third person' in the Luxemburg sense was to be expected in these capitalistic regions.

Moreover, he urges, there is nothing accidental about imperialism. The unfortunate Kautsky, who so often made

[1] Op. cit., p. 81.   [2] Ibid., p. 83.

himself the object of Lenin's dialectical marksmanship, had argued at one stage of his career[1] that other developments were conceivable; and that perhaps the monopolists of various countries might realize the dangers of warfare and come together in great international combinations, thus tremendously facilitating that painless transition to socialism for which he so fervently hoped. No such easy visions were acceptable to the founder of the Soviet Republic. It was not merely muddle-headed but positively ignoble to entertain them for a moment.

'Kautsky writes,' he says — one can almost hear the snarl of contempt with which he pronounced the opprobrious surname — 'Kautsky writes that, from the purely economic point of view, it is not impossible that capitalism will go through yet another phase, that of the extension of the policy of the cartels to foreign policy, the phase of ultra-imperialism, i.e. of a super-imperialism, a union of world imperialism and not struggles among imperialisms; a phase when wars shall cease under capitalism, a phase of the joint exploitation of the world by internationally united finance capital.

'. . . Kautsky's meaningless talk about ultra-imperialism encourages among other things that profoundly mistaken idea which only brings grist to the mills of the apologists of imperialism, *viz.*, that the domination of finance capital *lessens* the unevenness and contradictions inherent in world economy, whereas in reality it *increases* them.'[2]

Here then we have the main outlines of the central communist theory. It must be acknowledged at once that it is analytically possible. It is quite conceivable that in order to avoid a reduction in the rate of profit, groups of

[1] It is to be feared that no particular consistency is to be discovered in Kautsky's attitude. The detailed analysis of his work by Winslow and others reveals little but an interesting muddle.

[2] Op. cit., p. 87.

financiers might act in the way it suggests. It is not open to the logical objections which can be brought against most forms of the underconsumption theory. Nor can it be said to be concerned, as was that theory, with anything less than the main tendencies of capitalism. If financiers and monopolists act in the way suggested, it is not because of any incidental imperfection in the monetary mechanism. On the logical plane at least, its claim to be an indictment of a whole type of society is not inconsistent.

The question to be decided, therefore, is whether it fits the facts.

CHAPTER III

THE MARXIAN THEORY TESTED

1 *Criteria of Verification*

IN the last chapter, after a brief survey of the earlier forms which have been assumed by the theory that the root cause of war is the existence of capitalism, we examined in some detail that form which has now become the settled orthodoxy of communism, Lenin's theory of imperialism. We found that this theory suffered from none of the logical deficiencies to which its predecessors were subject and that it represented a coherent explanation of what might happen, if its assumptions corresponded with reality. In this chapter, therefore, we must proceed to inquire whether this correspondence is actually to be discovered. Does the Leninist theory fit the known facts of history? That is the question we have to answer.

Let us first remind ourselves shortly of the essential assumptions which it makes, the assumptions whose justification must be demonstrated if the hypothesis is to have validity. Broadly speaking there are two: firstly, the pressure of 'finance capital' operating through the mechanism of the export of capital; secondly, the inevitability and the universality of this type of causation within the period, let us say, since about 1870. Our task, therefore, is to discover whether, during this period, wars or the danger of war have actually been engendered by this mechanism and whether its operation has been sufficiently widespread to justify the claim that it has been all important.

To do this is necessarily a somewhat difficult matter, demanding at all stages a broad feeling for evidence and a strong sense of proportion. For, in the nature of things, we cannot hope to institute police court tests. We cannot call witnesses. We cannot even always examine all the documents. In any investigation of this sort we have to rely on a consensus of evidence which is necessarily fragmentary. There is thus always a possibility that documents which have not been published, witnesses who have not left records, might provide information invalidating our conclusions. There must necessarily be an element of conjecture in all verifications of this sort.

Realization of this, however, should not lead to a pedantic scepticism. We should not refuse to admit that a certain war was due to the pressure of high finance just because we cannot prove that Banker X (equipped with false beard) had secret confabulations with foreign minister Y at rendezvous Z. If there is a general body of evidence conducive to the belief that this kind of pressure was being applied, it would be absurd to deny the probability that that was one of the causes, even though the day-to-day movements of the leading actors cannot be traced. We must not shirk the formulation of general conclusions because we do not know everything.

Similarly, we must be on our guard against rejecting the allegation of this kind of causation because of the discovery that factors other than economic have also been operative. It is quite true that Lenin and his followers were both propagandists and philosophers and sometimes stated their views in forms so extreme that one would imagine that there was nothing in any war but the machinations of finance capital. But to imagine that their main position can be refuted by the discovery of exceptions to this, is to take the task of verification too easily. It is very hard to be fair to communists, for they are seldom fair to anyone else. But if we are to examine their views with the desire, not to make debating points but to get at the truth, we ought surely to admit that these extreme formulations are simply propagandist simplifications. We must not assume that Lenin was unaware of the operation of factors other than that particular economic factor which he diagnosed as the main culprit. We must assume that he knew that factors such as mob patriotism, historical prejudice, personal ambitions and the like are to be found mixed up with the history of almost any war, but that it was his contention that such factors were subsidiary to the operations of finance capital and in many cases, perhaps, consequential on these operations. And, if we are to judge him fairly, we must ask, not whether there were never any exceptions to his most crudely worded claims, but rather whether his general sense of proportion is justified. We must try to verify the most reasonable formulations of the theory, not the soapbox simplifications.

2 *Examples of Capitalist Imperialism*

It would be possible, I think, to make debating points regarding the role played in Lenin's detailed exposition by the peculiar concept of 'finance capital'. It was certainly not true, in the years before 1914, that the German banking system was at all typical of the systems prevailing in the other chief financial centres. In Great Britain, for instance, the capital exporter *par excellence*, the banks played little or no part in the conduct of industrial undertakings; and what industrial monopoly there was owed little to financial manipulations. *Finanzkapital*, in the Hilferding sense, was a chiefly German phenomenon; and if we were to demand strict accuracy at all points, we should have to regard it as militating considerably against the universality of Lenin's theory that it leans so heavily on this concept.

But it would be wrong to press this point very far. For, if, in countries other than Germany, there was not so much 'finance capital' as Lenin and Hilferding thought, there was certainly much capital export; and, in spite of much mystery mongering with 'finance capital', it is capital export which is really the central concept in the theory. If therefore for 'pressure of finance capital' we are content to write 'investment pressure' in general, the whole thing can be rephrased in terms of much greater plausibility. Investment capital in general includes 'finance capital'. If we regard this part of the theory as substantially verified where we find investment pressure, whether or not this is exerted through the special Hilferding mechanism, we give it more of a chance than it would have if we insisted on the narrow interpretation.[1]

Now it does not seem that there can be any doubt that, in certain cases, investment capital, in this wide sense, has played a major part in engendering diplomatic friction. We can find many instances in which governments have been the instruments of finance or have acted consciously on behalf of financial interests; and in some cases, this has resulted in war or acute danger of war. Against the smug respectability of latter day 'economic advisers', who would deprecate the suggestion that sectional interest can ever be sinister, the Marxian protest has abundant justification.

A classical example of this type of situation is afforded by the Boer War. Of course it would be a gross over-simplification to suggest that even here the process of causation was at all simple. It would be very silly to sug-

---

[1] It would also be possible to make extensive criticisms of Lenin's general views concerning monopoly. It is not at all clear that the natural tendency of all types of industry is always towards monopoly. But to discuss this at any length would interrupt the main argument which relates to the export of capital. I have set out my own views on the subject in an essay entitled 'The Inevitability of Monopoly' which is printed in my *Economic Basis of Class Conflict*, pp. 45-80.

gest that members of the British government were in the pay of the big gold-mining interests who wished to overthrow the Boer republic. We know, indeed, that the man whose policy did so much to make inevitable the final break, Alfred Milner, was a man of great integrity and public spirit, whose motives were much more influenced by the ideologies of empire and *realpolitik* which he had learned from German teachers, than by any particular regard for the capitalists of the Rand. It is doubtful whether even Rhodes, for all his financial interests, is to be regarded as predominantly out for gain; like many men who have made large fortunes rapidly when young, he was possessed in later life by grandiose visions of a quasi-religious nature which he was not unwilling to realize by harsh and unscrupulous means; and it is probable that in this instance, as in others, these were his main incentives. Moreover, large issues of state, unconnected with the position of the Uitlanders, were involved. The opening of the Delagoa railway was thought to menace the desired unification of South Africa. The rumours of a Boer plot, supported by a great continental power, may or may not have been justified. But, given the position of the British in Africa, there can be no denying that the policy of Kruger must have been a cause for grave misgiving.

In spite of this, when every allowance has been made for these complications, it does not seem possible to deny that it was the investments on the Witwatersrand and the pressure from their owners which played the leading role. The Jameson Raid may or may not have been connived at by the British government. But it was planned by Rand capitalists; and the fact that it was so planned must be a central feature of any explanation of the relations between the Boer and the British governments in the period between the Raid and the final declaration of hostilities.

Moreover, when all due regard has been paid to the larger issues involved in the negotiations concerning the Uitlander Franchise and the way in which these issues were conceived by Chamberlain and Milner, the fact remains that the negotiations were concerned with the position and the interests of foreign investments and investors; and that if it had not been for these interests they would not have taken place at all. It is doubtful how far the position of the Rand interests corresponds to the ideal type of 'finance capital' as conceived by Lenin and Hilferding. But it would be sheer pedantry to make this an excuse for evading the conclusion that, taken by and large, the whole incident is an excellent example of the way in which pressure from foreign investors can lead to international war.[1]

This example is not isolated. Scrutiny of the diplomatic history of the last sixty years discloses many cases in which governments have acted on behalf of capitalists who have made investments in foreign countries and a number of cases in which such pressure has led to severe diplomatic friction and military action. German action in regard to Samoa, American action in regard to Haiti, British and German action in regard to Venezuela — such are cases in which, whatever the penumbra of other factors, the leading role of investment interest seems reasonably well authenticated.[2] In such cases we must surely agree that, sympathetically interpreted, this part of Lenin's theory does correspond with the facts.

---

[1] Readers who are inclined to regard this as too one-sided an account are requested to postpone final judgment until chap. v, sect. 2, where an attempt is made to do justice to certain other aspects of the problem.

The literature of this subject is enormous. An excellent short account of the main issues involved is given in LANGER, *The Diplomacy of Imperialism*, chaps. viii and xviii.

[2] See STALEY, *War and the Private Investor*, especially chaps. v and vii.

3 *Some Alleged Cases Further Examined*

But Lenin's theory is not confined to the assertion that cases can be found in which the interests of investors have been the main cause of diplomatic friction. It asserts further that, in the period since capitalism has become 'mature', a mechanism of this sort has been the main cause of all, or at least a majority of international disputes and encounters. The peculiar characteristic of the theory is, not that it asserts that the pressure of capital exporters may sometimes lead to war — many others have recognized that — but rather the claim that this is *the* typical situation. It would be unfair to argue that this contention would be invalidated if one or two exceptions could be found to this rule. But it is essential, if it is to be established, that it should be shown to be usually applicable. It is essential that the tendencies, of which the Boer War may be taken as a typical example, should be shown to be characteristic of the majority of cases in this period.

In fact, however, this demonstration does not seem to be possible. The cases that are often claimed as examples of such tendencies show, on examination, characteristics of quite a different order. The part played by finance in the major diplomacy of the period preceding the Great War, proves to be in the main, quite different from that postulated by the theory. We find indeed that where the relations of strong capital-exporting and weak capital-importing states are concerned, there governments have from time to time exerted pressure on behalf of investors. But where the relations of strong states are concerned, directly or indirectly, there the belief that the initiative comes from finance, or is exerted on behalf of finance, seems to rest upon misapprehension.

Let us look further at a few of the cases which the exponents of this theory usually cite as evidence.

Perhaps the most outstanding of these is the Russo-Japanese War of 1904. The interpretation commonly put forward is that the root cause of this conflict was the desire of the Russian government to safeguard the interests in certain Yalu timber estates of a group of investors in close touch with the Russian court. 'It was neither the Russian people nor the Russian bureaucracy which had determined to keep the Yalu district and to fight Japan for its possession,' says Mr. Brailsford. 'The resolution to possess it came from a little group of interested courtiers who were using the natural resources to further their private financial ends.[1]

This view, however, is not tenable. The researches of Professor Langer have brought to light information which to all candid minds must compel a conclusion almost exactly the opposite to that which is reached by the advocates of the theory of economic imperialism.[2] It is quite true that a group of courtiers were actively engaged in promoting a belligerent policy. It is quite true that they owned concessions in the Yalu area. But it is not true that their motives were economic. It is abundantly clear that the economic interest was a mere blind. There is in existence a document drawn up by the promoters of the enterprise in which the whole plan is set forth. It was desired to prevent concessions in this area coming into the hands of international syndicates on the ground that that would involve a fatal curtailment of Russian political ambitions. An East Asiatic company was to be set up, not aiming at immediate dividends, which should 'render a service to the tsar', foreign capital being perhaps admitted as a screen. A 'fighting vanguard disguised as lumbermen'

[1] H. N. BRAILSFORD, *The War of Steel and Gold*, 9th edition, pp. 51-2.
[2] *Europäische Gespräche*, Hamburg, IV (June 1926), pp. 279-322. See also STALEY, op. cit., pp. 55-62. Throughout the whole of this section I have drawn very heavily upon Mr. Staley's invaluable book.

were to be deployed on the concessions on the pretence of economic exploitation.

This in fact is what happened. In the face of the opposition of Witte and the moderates, the extremist groups succeeded in obtaining the support of no less a person than the Tsar himself. Two million roubles were appropriated from secret service money to assist the mock undertaking. Military roads were constructed and barracks disguised as timber warehouses were erected. 'An American who visited the scene . . . wrote that the one hundred Russians' who were supervising the activities of the labourers, 'with one or two exceptions were all military men.'[1] It is not surprising that it was not long before warfare began between the Japanese and the Russian timbermen.

Thus the pressure of investment capital proves in this case to have been a pure disguise for the operations of mystical Russian imperialism.

A somewhat similar case is presented by the history of the Turco-Italian War of 1911-12. Here again it is commonly asserted that a war was caused by the intervention of a government on behalf of investment capital — in this case the Banco di Roma. Here again, on examination, the actual relation involved between government and finance proves to be more or less exactly the opposite to what is commonly asserted. Mr. Staley, who has examined this case in detail, has no difficulty in showing that the annexation of Tripoli was projected by Italian statesmen long before the Banco di Roma had anything to do with the country. He shows too that the bank's decision to go at all was the result of an incentive offered by the Italian government, the privilege of rediscount facilities at the bank of Italy, and that it received further compensation in the shape of a subsidy to its navigation service. There

[1] STALEY, op. cit., p. 61.

was no lack of opening for surplus capital in Italy; and investments in Tripoli were subject to considerable risks for very poor returns. It is clear that, as in the case of the Yalu concessions, the economic interest created by the financial operations were merely a screen for political ambitions having little or no connection with the returns in which high finance is interested. The Italian government was anxious to find some offset to the loss of prestige which it had experienced at the battle of Adowa; and the occupation of Tripoli, facilitated by bargains with the French arising from the Morocco dispute, offered a suitable opportunity. That, once it was installed, the bank was not loath to claim the full measure of support which had been promised it and that it was even at pains to arouse public opinion in its favour, is a minor complication. In the inception of the enterprise and in the part played subsequently the role of finance was essentially that of agent.

Another famous example is the case of the Bagdad railway concessions. Disputes about these never actually led to war. But, in that type of literature which is apt to attribute the outbreak of wars in general to the operations of sinister interest, the whole episode has always loomed large as an example of the way in which the struggles of high finance for spheres of influence exacerbated international relations and prevented the sort of agreement which might have avoided the catastrophe of the Great War.

Now the complications of this dispute are endless and the motives involved are much more difficult to disentangle than in the instances we have already examined.[1] Perhaps we ought to begin by stating clearly that, at certain junctures, pressure from people with economic

[1] The whole episode is treated at length in EARLE, *Turkey, the Great Powers and the Bagdad Railway*. For the earlier incidents the chapters in LANGER'S *Diplomacy of Imperialism* are very helpful.

interests was actually attempted. Certainly, during the time when British public opinion was most interested in the question, propaganda on behalf of the Lynch Brothers, whose navigation rights on the Euphrates were said to be menaced, was very active and vociferous. It is extremely doubtful how far the attitude of the British Foreign Office was ever influenced by all this; the evidence points in the other direction. But discussion in the House of Commons definitely paid attention to these claims.

Nevertheless, to suggest that the main course of the dispute arose from the pressure of economic interests is to lose all sense both of fact and perspective. It is well known that the German bankers originally involved were highly reluctant to apply for the concessions and only proceeded to do so after strong pressure from the German government. It is established, too, that they were very willing to admit the participation of capital from other centres. And on the British side, it is notorious that the financiers interested were willing again and again to settle with the Germans and indeed had to be held back from doing so by pressure from the Foreign Office. Years before the foreign offices had adjusted their differences, the international bankers were in agreement.

As a matter of fact, the more one examines the history of this episode, the clearer it becomes that, although the dispute involved concessions which were essentially economic in character, the underlying motives of the governments concerned were predominantly diplomatic and strategic. The Russian objections to the German concessions were clearly of this order. No damage to Russian financial interests was conceivable from the development of Asia Minor and the Euphrates valley. The French motives are less clear. It is very probable that regard was paid to the interests of the French capital already invested in Turkey; it would not be at all surprising to find direct evidence of this. But diplomatic support of Russia seems also to have been an important motive; the French attitude here can only be thoroughly understood in the light of the general history of the development of the Russian Alliance. As for the British attitude, there can be little doubt that the main consideration was regard for the safety of communications with the East. The British Foreign Office was at first disposed to let the thing go through. But growing distrust of German ambitions, a distrust be it noted which finds justification in material which has since been published,[1] led to a change of view. It was not from a desire to forward the interests of British finance but to safeguard our position in the East that the Kaiser was given to understand that our objections would be waived if the section from Bagdad to Basra were in British hands. Whether, here as elsewhere, there were economic motives of a more general nature involved in all this diplomatic manœuvre is a question to which we shall have to return later. But there is little *prima facie* evidence which gives countenance to the Leninist hypothesis.

Finally, we may glance at the Morocco episode and the part said to be played by the Mannesmann interests. Here again we have an incident of critical importance in the diplomatic history leading up to the Great War, where it has become customary to allege that it was all due to the pressure of investment capital seeking profitable outlets abroad.[2]

---

[1] In the Willy-Nicky correspondence there is a letter from the Kaiser, written during the Boer War, in which he regrets that the railway had not yet been completed, since it would have 'offered the opportunity of despatching a few regiments from Odessa straight down to Koweet'.

[2] There is an excellent examination of the part played by the Mannesmanns in Mr. STALEY's book, op. cit., pp. 178 and 194. For a more general view of the whole Morocco friction, see SPENDER, *Fifty Years of Europe*, chap. xxxiii.

In this case it is well known that there was an extensive and influential agitation in Germany urging the government to take action to secure the operation of the concessions which, it was said, had been granted by the Sultan of Morocco to the representative of the Mannesmann firm. It is clear that this agitation played a part in poisoning good relations between the German and French governments and that the obstinacy of the Mannesmanns imposed difficulty after difficulty upon all who attempted to play the role of peacemakers. It is true that it has been urged in defence of the Mannesmanns that at first they were promised support by a German consul, and it may very well be that they had some genuine grievance. But it is established beyond doubt that they attempted to use governmental aid to forward their own interests and this in an area where international tension was already so great that the least friction was liable to set the whole diplomatic edifice alight. On any liberal or international-socialist theory of correct behaviour in economic relationships, their activities were mischievous and dangerous.

But before we conclude from this that the Mannesmanns' agitation occupies a central place in the history of the diplomacy of the period and that it furnishes an instance in any way typical for the Leninist theory, there are two not unimportant points to note.

In the first place, the Agadir crisis was nothing to do with the Mannesmanns. Apologies are perhaps due to people of good general education for mentioning this obvious fact; but we must not take much for granted nowadays. The Agadir crisis arose because the French proposed to take action against the local Sultan and the Germans were anxious to secure compensating concessions elsewhere. Conversations to this end had already been opened on a more or less friendly basis, when by one of those flashes of psychological insight so characteristic of German diplomacy, it occurred to Kiderlen-Waechter, the German minister involved, that it would facilitate matters if a gunboat were dispatched to Morocco. The whole thing was an obvious blunder on Kiderlen's part and need never have taken place had the negotiations been in the hands of anyone of even ordinary diplomatic finesse. In any case, the German objective was a slice of the Congo. The Mannesmanns were simply not in the picture.

Secondly, in so far as the Mannesmann agitation was a general cause of friction, it is to be observed that it was no affair of high finance. High finance in Germany was indeed scared stiff of Morocco. 'As soon as you mention Morocco', said a German secretary for foreign affairs, 'the banks all go on strike, every manjack of them.' The supporters of the Mannesmanns were, not the leaders of German finance, but Pan-German politicians — Navy League men, Junker reactionaries, romantic colonial enthusiasts. The Mannesmanns had indeed a clear economic interest. But, save in the case of the armament manufacturers subscribing to the Navy League,[1] the economic interest of their supporters, if they had an economic interest at all, was of a kind not disclosed by any analysis we have yet had occasion to examine.

[1] It is fairly generally accepted that for obvious reasons German armament manufacturers were heavy subscribers to the various militarist ideological organizations. But only those who know nothing of pre-war Germany will regard this as the moving impulse of these bodies. To ascribe the militarism of Wilhelmian Germany to the activities of armament manufacturers is about as sensible as to ascribe the National Socialism of Hitler to the industrialists who were silly enough to subscribe to party funds. Speaking generally, the influence of armament manufacturers in the causation of war has been enormously exaggerated. From time to time, certain groups may have succeeded in increasing the demand for their products. But to attribute the main demand to such influences is to lose all sense of probability and history. Governments which have relied upon state arsenals have not been more pacific than others.

4 *Finance and Diplomacy in the Modern Period*

Examples of this sort — and it would be very easy to multiply them extensively — are not merely interesting in themselves as outstanding cases where the communist writers misapprehend the actual facts, they also illustrate in various ways a relationship between governments and investors, which in the period under examination seems much more typical than that which is postulated by Lenin.

For, if we take a broad view of the main current of international relations in the period between 1870 and 1914, we find indeed that finance plays a not inconsiderable role.[1] But the nature of this role is almost precisely the reverse of that which we should expect from Marxian theory. In the relations, either direct or indirect, between strong states there is hardly any evidence of the influence of finance being used in a direction conducive to friction or war. There is hardly any evidence that high finance was an initiating factor in the complicated manœuvres of balance-of-power diplomacy. The one case which might at first sight be interpreted as an exception to this rule is British policy in regard to Egypt. But, as we shall note in the next chapter, even here there are other much more convincing explanations.

Against this absence of evidence of an active role on the part of high finance, there is abundant evidence of passive instrumentality. We do not find evidence that finance was often a prime mover. But there is plenty of evidence that finance was continually used as a pawn. This is perhaps not very conspicuous in the English scene where finance was usually more or less left to its own devices; although even here we have had occasion to observe the veto

[1] On all this see VINER, *International Finance and Balance of Power Diplomacy*, 1880-1914, 'The South-western Political and Social Science Quarterly', vol. IX, No. 4, March 1929. FEIS *Europe the World's Banker* should also be consulted.

imposed by the government in regard to the Bagdad railways. But, in Germany and France, government control of investment for diplomatic purposes was the usual thing. In the thrust and parry of balance-of-power diplomacy, the use of the financial weapon was taken as a matter of course.

Thus again and again we find instances of governments interfering to prevent the flow of capital going in a certain direction. The beginnings of the Franco-Russian *rapprochement* of the nineties, for instance, are to be traced, at least in part, to the veto imposed by Bismarck on loans to Russia from Germany. Similarly, at different times, for obvious diplomatic reasons, we find vetoes being imposed in Paris on lending to Italian and Central European enterprise. If it had not been for these vetoes, capital export would have taken these directions. The interests of finance, that is to say, lay in one direction; the interests of government in another.

Again we continually find governments actively promoting loans that would not otherwise have been made, in order to cement, or to forward, political alliances or ententes. We have already seen examples of this when examining Italian penetration in Tripoli and German exploitation of Asia Minor. The classical case, of course, is the case of the French loans to Russia. The Russian military railways were built by the savings of the French peasantry. There is no reason at all to suppose that French investment in Russia would have been on anything like the scale it actually assumed, had it not been for direct governmental encouragement. Similarly, at different times, we find Italy, now being wooed by German money, now being wooed by French. Again and again we hear of episodes where, before anything could be done by way of loans, appeals had to be made to the 'patriotism' of the local financial interests — perhaps not so difficult a virtue to exercise when disposing of other people's money.

'In all these transactions', says Professor Viner,[1] concluding his magisterial survey, 'the bankers seem to have been the passive and, in some cases, unwilling instruments of the diplomatists . . . Bankers rarely favour an aggressive policy towards powerful adversaries or even towards weaker countries if the latter have powerful friends. Whatever their attitude toward weak and friendless countries, in the diplomacy of the great powers they are a pacific influence. For the claim sometimes made that they exercised a controlling influence over pre-war diplomacy, the available source material offers not the slightest degree of support.'

Finally, we may make two general observations, which seem highly germane to any examination of the theory that imperialist expansion and international conflict are essentially the product of the struggles of finance to avoid a declining rate of profit.

On the one hand, there were areas of highly developed capitalism such as Holland, Switzerland and Scandinavia, which played no part whatever in the expansionist game. Of course there were obvious reasons why, *by themselves*, these countries would have been unable to play the game to much purpose. But if, as the Leninist theory alleges, the mechanism of the state is the willing instrument of finance capital, there is no reason why they should not have allied themselves with other more powerful allies to join in predatory enterprise. Capital was just as subject to the tendency to a declining rate of profit, in these countries, as elsewhere. Yet in fact they maintained a rigid non-expansionist neutrality.

On the other hand, two at least of the governments who

[1] Op. cit., p. 45.

were most conspicuous in the expansionist movement, were the governments of countries which were definitely borrowing areas. During the whole of this period, Russia and Italy were large importers of capital. Russian expansion was financed, first by German, then by French, money. Italy's share in the Bagdad Railway had to be taken up by Greek bankers. There can be no question in either of these cases of surplus capital unable to find profitable investment at home. Yet in both cases imperialist expansion was an extraordinarily active force. There is something here not accounted for by Lenin's theory.

5 *The Inadequacy of the Leninist Theory*

The conclusion of our investigation is unmistakable. It is quite probable that in many cases our survey is guilty of errors of emphasis and perspective. But unless the evidence of years of disinterested research on the part of the various authorities we have used is to be dismissed as hopelessly inaccurate and biased, the conclusion is surely established that the theory which we have examined does not stand up to the test of fact. There have been cases where the influence of investors and financiers has been, roughly speaking, as postulated by that theory. Any full survey of the facts must not leave these cases out of sight. But, in the main perspective, these cases are the exception. The more typical cases show other relationships not accounted for by this theory. There is no convincing evidence that it was the struggles of finance capital or the machinations of general investors which were responsible for the outbreak of the Great War.

And indeed, as one reads the literature of the theories of economic imperialism, one is sometimes tempted to ask whether its authors have ever so much as seen an animal of the species, banker. The picture drawn seems so different, the psychological attitude assumed so unlike anything that can normally be witnessed in the circles of high finance, that one feels that one has walked through the looking-glass into a world in which all one's usual estimates of men and the way they move have gone completely topsy-turvy. 'Does anyone seriously suppose', asks Mr. Hobson (seriously), 'that a great war could be undertaken by any European State, or a great state loan subscribed, if the house of Rothschild and its connections set their face against it?'[1] To which one can only answer, ruefully, that many people might seriously suppose it.

In fact the verdict of those who have known the financier best has always been in the opposite direction. Mr. Asquith's contemptuous description of the city magnates on the outbreak of the Great War is well known. Equally decisive and equally damaging to the assumptions of the Marxian theory is the judgment of Wolf-Metternich expressed, not in an utterance intended for public consumption, but in a confidential dispatch to von Bülow. 'High finance shakes its knees whenever any kind of political complications crop up'.[2] No doubt there have been financiers of a different moral calibre. But it has yet to be shown that they were anything but exceptions to the general run of their kind.

But what are we to conclude from all this? Are we to resign ourselves to the view that, save in the case of certain colonial expeditions, economic factors have played no part recently in the causation of diplomatic friction and war? Are we to conclude that it has been all just a question of high politics and that there is nothing more in it than that?

This does not follow at all. All that we have discovered

---

[1] *Imperialism*, 2nd edition, p. 57.
[2] Quoted by KANTOROWITZ, *The Spirit of English Policy*, p. 378.

so far is that the communist theory is unacceptable.[1] What we have now to do is to see whether it is not possible to construct a theory which provides a more satisfactory explanation of the facts.

---

[1] It is amusing to note that, with the conclusion of their non-aggression pact with the Soviet, something like this theory has been taken over by the Nazis. A Nazi journal is quoted by the *Daily Telegraph* (September 29th, 1939) as saying that the German army has now only one enemy, 'namely the British capitalist', who presumably, on true-blue Leninist lines, is to be conceived as aiming at the enhancement of monopoly profits by the destruction of German industry. Poor British capitalist, the only way in which history is likely to find him guilty for the present catastrophe is that, being rather stupid and very pacific, he failed to support effective action before the gangsters were strong enough to strike.

CHAPTER IV

THE ECONOMIC CAUSES OF WAR

1 *National Power and Economic Factors*

OUR researches thus far have had a negative outcome. We have surveyed the underconsumptionist versions of the communist theory of imperialism and found that they were either logically defective or that they did not prove their main contention. We have examined the Leninist theory that, in the most recent period of capitalism, war has been due to the activities of finance or investment capital and we have found that, although cases of this sort can be found, they are the exception rather than the rule. In the majority of cases, finance capital, if it has played a role at all, seems to have been instrument rather than impulse. It is now time to proceed to something more positive, to attempt to construct a theory more in harmony with correct economic analysis and with the facts.[1]

Let us start from the most obvious phenomena of international relations — diplomatic manœuvres, ententes, alliances, war. It is easy to see that, in their most general aspect, all these can be conceived as part of a perpetual struggle for power — a struggle either to conserve power or to increase it. Whatever view we may hold concerning the ultimate *raison d'être* of power, we can all agree that, in the day-to-day conduct of international relations, it is in terms of efforts to achieve this proximate end that most of the activities of the agents immediately concerned can

[1] Certain features of the theory here developed are to be found in my *Economic Planning and International Order*, and in an essay on 'The Economics of Territorial Sovereignty', reprinted in my *Economic Basis of Class Conflict*.

probably be most realistically summarized. There is no need to marshal detailed evidence. The whole body of diplomatic literature — state papers, ambassadors' dispatches, general staff memoranda — are couched in a language of which this is, so to speak, the permanent implicit major premise. Our object is to conserve (or increase) our power. Such and such an action will affect our power in such and such a way. This action is therefore to be commended (or rejected).

It should be clear that, in such considerations, economic factors are almost necessarily involved. The attainment of military power in the narrowest sense involves the control of scarce resources. The attainment of any kind of power, save perhaps the power of the spirit, is similarly conditioned. This is so whatever the social system of the state in question. Under socialism, as much as under capitalism, national power rests on economic factors.

Thus national power involves command of raw materials. If raw materials essential for the prosecution of war or for the general functioning of the economic system are situated in territories liable to be inaccessible in time of war, national power is substantially limited. It is all very well to argue that, *given peace*, the raw material problem is only a matter of tariffs and other barriers to trade; and that, *given an absence of restriction*, it does not exist at all. This is true enough. But the fact is that peace is not given and an absence of restriction cannot be assumed. The given fact of the world situation, as we have known it hitherto, is not peace but war and the danger of war; and, if raw material supplies are in the hands of powers with whom the state is likely to be at war, or from whose territories it may be cut off, then the preservation of national power must necessarily involve concern with the securing of adequate provisions.[1] This, of course, is the main explanation of the continual pre-occupation of certain modern powers, with the ownership or control of territories in which oil is situated. To the eye sophisticated by Marxian theory it seems to appear that the various manœuvres in this respect have been inspired solely by sinister interest. But this is most improbable. We do not know with any certainty how much sinister interest has been operative here; the material for sound judgment is not available. It is quite possible that there may have been most substantial rake-offs in particular cases. But, having regard to the importance of oil in naval and aerial warfare, to suppose that independent socialist states having to take account of the danger of war, would have manœuvred very differently, is to lack all sense of proportion.

In the same way, considerations of national power involve concern with command over communications. To safeguard supplies and to facilitate naval and military operations, ownership by the citizens of the state of certain important canals or railways may be regarded as funda-mental. We have seen already, in the case of the Bagdad railway, how considerations of this sort resulted in impedi-ments being placed on the agreement of financial syndi-cates. In spite of the not infrequent operation of sinister interest in this region, it is probable that similar considera-tions have played a large part in determining the long-run tendencies of United States policy in Central America.[2]

Less obvious, but no less important in this respect, is

---

[1] It is no accident that it is the powers who have most consciously regarded war as a permanent and justifiable instrument of national policy, who have always insisted that the raw material problem is not merely a problem of trade restrictions and monetary policy. The silence of the so-called permanently neutral states on this point is a most sig-nificant contrast.

[2] See ANGELL, *Foreign Economic Policy of the United States, passim.*

the role of other types of foreign investments. It is a great source of strength in war, and hence in diplomacy involving appeal to war, to have available extensive supplies of realizable foreign assets. The enormous strength of Great Britain in the Great War of 1914-18 owed much to the foreign investments of her citizens. To have an international money market within the borders of the state may have technical advantages of no small importance in the conduct of war and diplomacy. We have seen how such powers were exploited by France and Germany in the balance-of-power struggle between 1870 and 1914. Moreover, particular types of foreign assets may provide apt instruments for exercising particular kinds of diplomatic control and pressure. Disraeli's investment in Suez Canal shares is a classical instance of this kind;[1] and the great solicitude of British policy for Egyptian investments in general is probably to be explained in a similar manner.

All this is so important, if we are to understand what goes on in the foreground of diplomatic consciousness, that Mr. R. G. Hawtrey has been led to argue that it is futile to attempt to disentangle economic from other causes. 'The distinction between economic and political causes is an unreal one,' he says. 'Every conflict is one of power

---

[1] It is often said that the whole episode of British intervention in Egypt was dictated by the interests of British Bondholders; and advocates of a more or less Marxian interpretation of diplomacy (e.g. H. N. BRAILSFORD, *The War of Steel and Gold*) seem to regard the whole Egyptian episode as a classic case of aggressive economic imperialism. This is very unplausible. Nobody would wish to deny that some part was played by regard for the interests of investors. But it is very doubtful whether a succession of both liberal and conservative cabinets would have maintained a position of such extreme diplomatic embarrassment if it had not been for the overriding strategic considerations involved. The idea of Mr. Gladstone as the agent of Rothschilds and Barings can only be regarded as comic. On the history of the occupation of Egypt, probably the most solid and reliable account is to be found in LANGER, *European Alliances and Alignments*, chap. viii.

and power depends on resources.'[1] Power in Mr. Hawtrey's view is something ultimate; he even goes so far as to deny the possibility of interpreting the wars of nationalism in terms other than those of the struggle for power.

Now, as we have seen already, there is a plane of analysis on which power may very well be regarded as the objective most clearly aimed at. No one can study the detailed literature of diplomatic intercourse without coming to feel that, for many of the participants involved, the mere preservation or increase of power has become the only objective. The diplomatic game acquires a sort of independent status; and the wider forces involved may themselves be deflected by the skill, the mistakes or the idiosyncrasies of the participants. How much of the history of the world has been determined by influences of this sort is a question about which wise men may well differ. But no one who has attentively studied the facts will be inclined to minimize their significance. There is a real profundity in Mr. Hawtrey's remark that the principal cause of war is war itself. In the absence of the rule of law in international relations, a situation is created in which the maintenance or increase of power in the military sense is an almost inevitable objective of the conduct of independent governments.

Nevertheless, it is surely too drastic a simplification to regard the desire for power as being always a final objective. The foreign ministers and ambassadors who are the immediate agents in the detailed manœuvres of international relations, may from day to day think only in such undifferentiated terms; but the leaders of opinion, the representatives of various interests, not to mention the

[1] *The Economic Aspects of Sovereignty*, p. 120. I hope that my disagreement with Mr. Hawtrey on this particular point will not be thought to indicate an undervaluation of this brilliant and illuminating essay which must be a stimulus to all who read it.

introspective citizen, will certainly from time to time conceive the issues in terms of something more ultimate.
Power as such may indeed be an ultimate attraction;
we must never underestimate the extent of sheer irration-
ality which is operative in these large affairs. In the case
of a monomaniac like Hitler, it is obviously the governing
consideration. But sometimes, at least, somebody will
pause to ask what it is all about. Somebody will indicate
the further objectives for the realization of which national
power is essential. It is indeed extraordinarily difficult to
get a right sense of proportion here. But it is surely wrong
to suppose that such ultimate objectives are not often very
important. And it is surely wrong to argue that, because
the achievement of any kind of objective involves the use
of scarce resources, it is impossible to distinguish between
the economic motive, which is concerned with the enhancement of command of resources in general, and other
motives which are more specific in character.[1]

We may agree that the diplomatic struggle is a struggle
for power. We may agree that all struggles for power
involve the control of scarce resources. But this does not
relieve us from proceeding to ask the questions: for what
purpose is national power wanted? Are these purposes
economic or non-economic in character?

2 *Non-economic Motives and War*

It is no object of the present analysis to deny the
importance of motives which are non-economic.

There does not seem the slightest reason to suppose that
motives of this sort have not often been very powerful.
Lust for personal aggrandizement, desire for liberation
from a foreign yoke, zeal for the principles of particular
religions, violent manifestations of mass hatred — what

[1] See Appendix, sect. 4, below.

serious student of history would wish to minimize the part which has been played by such factors in causing conflict through the ages? Of course it is very silly always to believe the apologia of official and other sources; the more sinister the cause, the greater the necessity for appeal to moral principles. But it is equally silly to postulate in advance that no declaration of purpose which does not conform to a certain preconceived pattern, the desire for wea'th in general, can ever possibly be true. It is childish to believe that we are always told the truth. But it is equally childish to believe that we are always told lies. If we look candidly at our own experience, we must surely realize that conflict between the men and the groups we have known is often concerned with matters not remotely connected with wealth, that it is simply fantastic to assert that motives are always economic or spring always from economic influences. What possible reason is there to assume that things become entirely different when the relations of historic persons and historic groups are in question?

It is probable, I think, that the fashion for interpreting everything in terms of economic causes has already become a little *démodé*. To the frustrated idealism of the dog days after the Great War of 1914-18 it was perhaps a perverse satisfaction to trace everything in a base world to 'merely' economic influences; to accept the analysis which purported to do so seemed a sign of superior sensitiveness. But it was never very sensible to do so; and events since those days have done much to remind us that many things other than the desire for wealth may move men to violent action. There are, of course, all sorts of motives mixed up in the present European struggle. As we shall see later on, there are economic motives involved which must not be underrated. But to regard the Nazi madness as being principally economic in nature is surely to invert the perspective.

There are, no doubt, decent and sincere people who still believe the whole Hitlerian upheaval to be a gigantic plot of the German heavy industries — yet another manifestation of 'the dying struggles of monopoly capitalism'. But this belief has been always rather *a priori* in character, and, as time goes on, it becomes more and more in contradiction with obvious facts.

But for all this, economic motives do play an important part in everyday human relations; and, as we shall see, there is every reason to suppose that they have often played an important and perhaps even a predominant part in the causation of certain historical conflicts. In providing explanations of how they may act and how in fact they have acted, we are not denying the role of other motives. We are not making any claims concerning their relative importance in 'history as a whole' — an absurd and impossible concept. We claim only that there are certain possible causes of conflict which are best conceived in terms of economic motives and important cases in history in whose explanation such conceptions seem to play an essential part.

3 *Sectional Interests and War*

Let us begin with the simplest examples. In the course of our examination of Marxian theory, we have observed cases in which war has been waged on behalf of particular private interests. It is not correct to infer from this, as the Marxians do, that they were waged in the interests of whole categories of economic factors — investment capital, trading capital or the like. It is not in the least clear, for instance, that investment capital in general, or even in Great Britain, had any direct material interest in the prosecution of the Boer War. What benefits one group of investors is not necessarily beneficial at all to others; and there is indeed reason to suppose that, where special groups of property owners (or, for that matter, workers) are given monopolistic privilege, the interests of the rest are directly damaged. What we need here is, not a concept of class interest in the sociological sense, but a concept of group interest in the sense of the theory of markets or the general theory of taxation. If we can find groups with similar interests of this kind, we are entitled to suspect a certain solidarity and to attribute to the group, as such, a pivotal position in the causal mechanism.[1] The common interest is obvious and tangible.

The best examples of the operation of this kind of influence are to be found in the history of the illiberal societies of earlier times. In the times of the absolute princes, for example, the prince himself and his immediate entourage had often a direct economic interest in the extension of territory. Not only did such extensions bring more glory — a non-economic consideration — they also brought more taxes, more dues, more lands — considerations which were decidedly economic. There can be no doubt, for instance, that William of Normandy had much to gain in this way by the conquest of England. There is no need to multiply examples; the history of such times is one continuous demonstration of the importance of this kind of thing.

Similarly, and perhaps even more significant, in the so-called mercantilist period, when the national states had emerged from the exclusive control of the monarch, the conduct of foreign relations was continually influenced by powerful groups of merchants having common interests in the monopoly of certain markets and opportunities of

---

[1] For a fuller treatment of the distinction between groups as constituted by market interest and statistical or sociological classes see my *Economic Basis of Class Conflict*, pp. 1-28.

plunder. Who can deny the economic motive operative in the conquest of British India — the rape of the Begums of Oude, the general policy of the East India Company? Again and again the great statutory monopolies of those days exercise an influence on policy which in fact conforms more or less to the model set up by the Marxians for the explanation of the history of a later period. It was of this period that Adam Smith wrote that 'commerce which ought naturally to be, among nations, as among individuals, a bond of union and friendship, has become the most fertile source of discord and animosity. The capricious ambition of kings and ministers has not, during the present and the preceding century, been more fatal to the repose of Europe, than the impertinent jealousy of merchants and manufacturers'.[1]

When we come to modern times, however, the importance of this kind of crude mechanism in the causation of actual war is a matter of much greater dubiety. We have seen already that cases of this sort are to be found. Moreover, there was an influential school of thought in Germany which idealized the policies of the mercantilist period and created an atmosphere in which the operations of sinister interest, never more at home than under the institutions of mercantilism, were clothed with an air of respectability. There can be no doubt that this intellectual influence, which ranged far beyond the frontiers of the Bismarckian Reich, did much to promote national policies which, in indirect ways which we shall be describing later on, were extremely conducive to conflict. But of direct manipulation of diplomacy by predatory traders and financiers there was much less than in earlier times. We must not underestimate the absolute amount of misery caused by those minor colonial expeditions where traders

[1] *Wealth of Nations*, Cannan's ed., vol. I, p. 457.

and governments worked hand in hand. But in the broad perspective of the general history of the age, their comparative significance is not great. To explain recent history largely in terms of the direct influence of aggressive sinister influence does not seem to be warranted by the facts.

4 National Interests and War

We have not by any means finished with the influence of sinister interest: it proves in the end to play a larger part than might appear at this stage of the argument.[1] But before developing this part of our theme any further, it will be found more convenient to pass on to consider the wider question of the influence of the economic interests of whole nations. We have noted ways in which the interests of industrial or commercial groups may lead to international conflict. Are there not ways in which the interests of whole geographical groups may be conceived to lead in the same direction?

Now, of course, interest has a subjective aspect. We may be able to make a rough guess in pounds, shillings and pence of the amount which may be gained or lost by a certain course of action. But whether such gains and losses will be considered worth the cost of the ardours and miseries of war depends upon the individuals concerned; and obviously their estimates may vary greatly. To the wretched neurotic who has just released chaos on Europe, the value of human life as compared with the achievement of his diseased aims is obviously very little. To some men of more sensitive conscience, almost any sacrifice may be better than the shedding of blood. Fortunately we are not called upon here to decide these nice moral issues. All that we need to ask is whether for nations as a whole there can be said to be objective gains or losses

[1] See chap. v, sect. 3, below.

which it is possible to conceive being balanced against whatever estimate is made of the cost, and whether it is plausible to suppose that such considerations have ever had historical importance. We are concerned, not with the question whether, in the ultimate sense, fighting is ever worth while, but simply with the question whether there can be shown to exist economic interests affecting the majority of national groups about which they may think it worth while to fight.

In earlier times and under primitive conditions there are plenty of examples of this sort of thing. We do not know exactly the origin of the barbarian invasions of the Roman Empire, whether it was the drying up of Asia, or pressure of population, or a mere continuation of ancient habits. But we can be fairly sure that the main purpose of the invading hordes was to better their condition. The children of Israel may have left Egypt because of the persecution of Pharaoh. But they invaded Palestine because it was a land which was flowing with milk and honey.

And, speaking generally, we may say that, wherever the extension of territory offers the opportunity of the appropriation of material factors of production or the enslavement of the inhabitants, it is possible that there may exist a national interest of this kind. This possibility has two forms. Either the members of the invading group may have the expectation of themselves *individually* obtaining land and booty. The wars of the early American settlers against the Indians are an obvious example of this. Or they may hope *collectively* to enjoy the ownership and usufruct of resources in the new possessions. The Romans, who exacted tribute from conquered territories, had an interest of this sort; and it is easy to see that, under totalitarian collectivism, similar interests may arise.

In recent history, however — and it is always recent

history which is the main focus of our attention — the annexation of territory has not usually carried with it, either the imposition of permanent tribute or the appropriation (either individual or collective) of human or material factors of production. In consequence, at first sight, it is more difficult to see how a nation as a whole can ever be conceived to have an economic interest in the extension of its existing territorial boundaries. Professor Schumpeter indeed has argued that war for this purpose can never be in the interests of the majority of the members of capitalistic societies.[1] In such societies, he thinks, the urge to war, in so far as it is at all general, is a sort of psychological atavism — a reversion to the ways of thought of the times of the absolute princes when the economic interests of the narrow class of rulers were clearly favoured by expansion.

There is much weight in this contention. The history of modern times shows many instances in which whole peoples have apparently been willing and sometimes even anxious to go to war in cases where there could be no gain in the economic sense for any but a tiny minority. The Italian wars for Tripoli and Abyssinia are obvious examples of this. The urge to destruction which seems to be so deep rooted a constituent of the unconscious mind is rationalized in childish and atavistic terms.[2] When we think of 'our country' conquering new 'possessions', unless we have been greatly sophisticated by the study of economics, we tend to think of some vast accretion to our own personal wealth and happiness quite disproportionate to the total resources involved. It is unfortunately only a very sophisticated man who would not feel that his

[1] *Zur Soziologie der Imperialismen*, 'Archiv für Sozialwissenschaft und Politik', xlvii, 1918-19, pp. 1-39, 275-310.
[2] An interesting study of these mechanisms is to be found in Durbin and Bowlby, *Personal Aggressiveness and War*.

country was materially better off if he read that it had annexed the North Pole.

Moreover, it is also to be remembered that the thinkers who provided the main rationalization for the new imperialism of the eighties and the nineties, were men who had grown up in an atmosphere in which the intellectual habits of the *absolut Fürstentum* had never been shaken off. The main school of German economists of that period, who unquestionably were the originators of the whole movement, were the lineal descendants of the old cameralists whose whole object in life was to instruct the prince how to increase the revenues of his estate.[1] To

---

[1] The importance in recent European history of the reactionary literature of the German social sciences is so considerable that any attempt to explain the general evolution of policy which fails to take account of it, is bound to be out of proportion. In English-speaking countries, our natural aversion from the pretentious and our ingrained unwillingness to read the less elegant of the foreign tongues has resulted in an ignorance of the German intellectual atmosphere of the last seventy years which has distorted our view of history and which even prevented us understanding Hitler until it was too late to avoid catastrophe. It is significant that, in PROFESSOR LANGER'S *Diplomacy of Imperialism*, the most extensive and reliable work on the important diplomatic developments of the nineties, the chapter which deals with the intellectual foundations of imperialism is devoted to an account of the essentially derivative English movement; the German literature is only touched upon incidentally in other chapters. This seems to show as apt a sense of proportion as a work which, purporting to explain the art of the high Renaissance, devoted its main analysis to the works of Italianate French painters. It would be easy to show in detail the personal connection with Germany of the intellectual leaders of English Imperialism. But Professor Langer is only representative of most of the members of his craft in Anglo-Saxon countries, who have nearly burst blood vessels in the honourable attempt to judge impartially the detailed diplomatic documents, while remaining almost completely anaesthetic to the differences of intellectual atmosphere amid which they were written. A distinguished exception to all this is PROFESSOR SONTAG'S admirable *Germany and England*. But even Professor Sontag does not seem to me quite to have realized the significance for international relations of the difference between English liberalism and German neo-mercantilism. English liberalism, with all its deficiencies, envisaged a world in which it was conceivable that all nations might live peacefully together. The world of German neo-mercantilism was a world in which such relations were necessarily excluded. Only the domination of the world by one power could bring peace under such a system.

such men the very idea of the liberal society with its strict distinctions between territory and property was something which was essentially alien. They never understood liberalism and they never wanted to understand it. The concept of the 'dominions' of the Emperor, which, to the cultivated minds of the western world, had become a ceremonial fiction symbolizing chiefly a certain spiritual unity, for them stood for what they conceived as the most important concrete reality; and to this frame of mind, the necessity for territorial expansion seemed one of the main requisites of policy. Professor Schumpeter, who of course knew these people well, is quite right in insisting upon the great importance of such ideas upon public opinion and policy. The atavistic delusions of the German *clercs* bear a heavy responsibility before history.

Nevertheless, it does not seem correct to contend that for the government of any particular state, sincerely anxious to forward the welfare of the citizens, the idea of a national economic interest in the maintenance and enlargement of the area of sovereignty is necessarily at all a delusion. On the contrary, in certain cases at least, it can be shown to be an interest which may be regarded as absolutely fundamental. Both in regard to trade and in regard to migration there may be very real national interests in the actual position of the boundaries.

Let us look first at trade; for, in the period before the Great War, this probably was the more important consideration.

It is not impossible to gain directly from aggression, even though no confiscation of property or imposition of tribute is involved. If the inhabitants of the conquered territories are prevented from selling their goods in markets other than those of the conquerors and if at the same time they are prevented from buying save in imperial markets, it is quite conceivable that the inhabitants of the dominant area may get advantages in the terms of trade. That is to say, they may get imports on cheaper terms. There is no doubt about this possibility. The free trade analysis which shows that, for the inhabitants of the imperial area as a whole, impediments to trade are likely to be disadvantageous, is not relevant here; for not all the inhabitants of that area are considered. It may well be that, in an empire practising this kind of colonial exploitation, all the inhabitants taken together can be regarded as being less well off than they would be in the absence of restriction. But this does not prevent the inhabitants of the metropolitan area making gains at the expense of the inhabitants of subordinate areas. It is not a question whether the total imperial income is likely to be raised by such measures. It is only a question whether the income of the dominant group can be so raised; and there is nothing in the economic theory underlying the general free trade position, which would lead us to regard this as impossible. For the last hundred years English-speaking economists have not speculated extensively upon this possibility. For, since the breakdown of the old colonial system and the emergence of the policy of free trade, the idea of exploiting the inhabitants of colonial territories in this way for the benefit of the inhabitants of the metropolitan area has become increasingly antipathetic.[1] But, among the less squeamish political philosophers of Central Europe, it is this type of policy which has always been envisaged, when colonies were being demanded. What German colonial enthusiast ever contemplated that the inhabitants of

---

[1] Since the abandonment of the free trade system and the imposition in certain parts of the empire of virtual prohibition on trade with Japan there has been some backsliding here.

subject areas should be free to trade with other empires?[1]

But while there undoubtedly exists the possibility of this kind of gain from aggression, there are many reasons for believing that, in fact, the extent to which it would be likely to be realized is much more limited than has often been supposed. Unless the subjection of the colonies is to be absolutely rigid, there will be a tendency to ease their situation by compensating advantages in the metropolitan area. The inhabitants of the metropolitan area will be tied to the colonies as the inhabitants of the colonial area are tied to them. And, in such a case, the general free trade analysis begins to become more and more relevant. The more restrictions are imposed, the more both areas tend to lose. The history of the old colonial system, which was supposed to be run on these mutual benefit lines, does not lead to high hopes concerning the eventual benefit to the inhabitants of a metropolitan area of any closed colonial system where the inhabitants of the colonies are not virtually enslaved. Moreover, even if the economic limitations are all on one side, that is to say, if the metropolitan area imposes a completely selfish will on the colonies, it must be remembered that the financial costs of enforcing such a policy may very easily more than

[1] It is this difference of political assumption which has led to such complete failure of English and German economists to understand each other on this matter. The English, never dreaming that among civilized peoples, it would be thought respectable to regard the inhabitants of colonial territories merely as instruments, and, knowing from general analysis that, for the Empire as a whole, the effect of such measures would probably be adverse, have been apt to regard the Germans as deficient in analytical insight. The Germans, suffering from no such inhibitions and scenting the prospect of sectional gains of the kind to which their *Kartellpolitik* had made them well accustomed, could not understand why the English should be concerned to deny their possibility. If one understands the difference of assumption, the logical contradictions disappear. But it does not seem as though such differences would be very susceptible of settlement after 'full and frank discussion at an international conference'.

offset any general gains through the terms of trade. If the costs of administration are high, then particular industrial and commercial groups within the metropolitan area may continue to benefit. But the main body of the people are unlikely to be better off.

For these reasons it does not seem as though there can be said to exist for the majority of geographical groups a very strong objective interest of this kind in the gains of aggression. It is possible that the belief that such an interest exists may have often influenced policy. But, given the assumptions of civilized people concerning what is legitimate in the treatment of dependencies, and given the disposition of the dependencies to make trouble if they are exploited, it can legitimately be argued that the possible gains of aggression are not often such as to be likely to be thought worth the candle. They are not analytically impossible. They are not impossible to completely ruthless conquerors. But, in the world in which we lived before the advent of Hitler, it is doubtful whether they were practically very significant.

On quite a different footing, however, is what may be called the defensive interest. There may not be much to be *gained directly* by a restrictionist imperialism. But there may be much to *lose* from the restrictionist policies of other powers. A very simple contrast will make this abundantly plain.

Let us suppose in the first place that as a part of a general world settlement, Great Britain were to hand over her existing colonial empire to an international authority, which proceeded thereafter to administer these territories on free trade open door lines. On such an assumption, it is hard to believe that many Britishers would be economically damaged. There might be some slight loss to the educated classes due to the widening of the competition

77

for openings in the colonial service. There might be some loss to contractors who, under British jurisdiction, enjoyed advantages as regards government business.[1] Speaking generally, however, on the assumption of the maintenance in perpetuity of these principles of international administration, it is highly improbable that the average man or woman would be any worse off. It is probable indeed, if a similar sacrifice were to be made by other nations that, in the end, the general standard would be raised.

But curtailments of territory are not usually of this nature. Hitherto in the history of the world, they have usually involved transfers, not to impartial international authorities, but to powers practising restriction of trade. If this is the case, then the outcome may be very different. Let us suppose that Great Britain were defeated in war and stripped of her colonial possessions by a power which proceeded to surround these territories with restrictions on trade with other areas. That surely would be a catastrophe of the first order of magnitude, a catastrophe affecting not merely the incomes of particular groups of property owners and workers but the income of the nation as a whole.[2] Markets which before were open to us, would now be closed. We should sell our goods, and hence the services of our factors of production, on terms

[1] It is possible that the abolition of the recently imposed preferential system might mean some slight adverse turn in the general terms of trade. But I think this is highly improbable.

[2] It is a curious thing that such a possibility does not appear to have entered the minds of Marxian writers. Marxian writers have indeed made much of the possibility of aggressive colonization. They have shown — it is one of the most valuable and courageous parts of their analysis — the possibility that 'aristocracies' of labour may share with capital the gains of colonial exploitation. But they have not seen the common interests of national groups in resisting the curtailment of markets. Here, as elsewhere, their failure to realize the sociological significance of immobility of labour has blinded them completely to causes of conflict cutting right across the horizontal class divisions of society.

less favourable than before. A general reduction of the standard of living would be inevitable. Such dangers are not imaginary. The inhabitants of Great Britain have fortunately not yet been called upon to suffer such great calamities. But elsewhere in recent history we can find most conspicuous examples. The economic organization of pre-war Austria, especially Vienna, was keyed up to supply the needs of the vast area of the old Austrian Empire. Suddenly, as it were overnight, the greater part of this market was cut off by almost prohibitive tariffs. The territorial division of labour of the Danube basin was destroyed by nationalist particularism; and the unfortunate Austrians, in particular the inhabitants of Vienna, had to accommodate themselves to a market which could only absorb their products at a reduction of values (and hence real incomes) which was catastrophic. We all know the results for that gracious and elegant civilization of this process of strangulation. It is not difficult to understand that, if successful war could have prevented it, that might easily have been regarded as a price well worth the paying.[1]

Much the same sort of considerations apply in regard to migration. So long as there are no restrictions on migration into other areas, the inhabitants of any particular area are not poorer because the territories ruled over by their government are not larger. They may think it is a hardship that, in order to improve their position, they have to move into areas under other flags. But this is

[1] By this I do not wish to say anything to extenuate the course which was actually followed by the diplomacy of pre-war Austria. The remedy was not Conrad's preventive war, but some form of federal constitution which would have averted the threatened disintegration. But I think that it has been a dim perception of the essentially defensive foundations of Austrian aggression which, even during the worst periods of war-time hatred, made our attitude to old Austria essentially different from our attitude to Wilhelmian Prussia.

not an economic interest in the sense in which we have defined it; and it is not an interest which prevented millions of Europeans in the times of freedom of movement from moving to more spacious horizons. But if migration is blocked, if the inhabitants of the less congested national areas refuse to admit immigrants from more congested parts, then there may be a real conflict of national interests. The plea for *Lebensraum* has often been the disguise for other more sinister intentions. But no candid person can deny that, when freedom of movement is suspended, the problem is real and urgent.

5 *Historical Observations: England and Germany*

Here surely we have the outlines of a theory which affords a much more plausible explanation of the economic causes of the diplomatic struggles of the modern period than any other we have yet examined. Whether or not foreign ministers and ambassadors often thought in these terms, here, if they had reflected, there was a permanent justification for maintaining and increasing national power. It was a justification, too, which could vindicate insistence on petty points which in themselves involved no grave economic injury. If, by a series of small losses, the general standing of the nation were weakened, then there was danger of the 'catastrophe' so often vaguely alluded to, the substantial loss of prestige and influence which might carry with it the danger of exclusion and impoverishment. So long as other powers practised exclusion, so long there was danger of substantial damage from alterations of national boundaries. It is unlikely that the rationale of policy was frequently stated in these particular terms; public apologia were more apt to rely on the more grandiose imagery of power. But if a cross-examiner had pressed sufficiently persistently the naive question 'Why do we want to maintain our power?' it is probable that, sooner or later, such an explanation would have been forthcoming.

It is an explanation furthermore which, better than any other, fits the facts of the scramble for colonies. During the period in which this took place Great Britain was the only great power which did not practise a policy of commercial restriction. The British colonial empire was run on free trade principles. But the other powers pursued other policies. It followed therefore that, for any one power, if any of the others, save great Britain, 'got there first', there was a loss of potential markets; and of course there was always the danger, more feared at that time than was necessary, that British policy might turn restrictionist. Hence there was a real national interest in expansion; an interest, be it noted, not confined to the propertied classes. Working people, equally with capitalists, stood to lose from the narrowing of potential markets.[1] With the recrudescence of protectionism in the seventies, the division of the world's surface between the different nations, which in the period of Cobdenism had seemed likely to become a matter of smaller and smaller importance, once more became a matter of real concern to responsible national leaders.

This is plain enough in the history of British colonial expansion. Undoubtedly, from time to time, particular annexations were supported by particular groups of interests. But the main object of the policy of successive governments was to prevent a curtailment of the market. Committed, as they were, to the principles of free trade, they had no desire to exclude other people. But they had every reason to fear that, if other people were in first,

---

[1] Indeed they stood to lose more, for capital was more mobile than labour.

they themselves would be found shut out.[1] Even an historian, so obviously unsympathetic to the British position as Professor Langer, admits this. 'With the setting aside of large parts of the unclaimed world as French and German Colonies', he says, 'there was an obvious danger that the British Market would be steadily restricted. Hence the emergence and sudden flowering of the movement for expansion. The English felt that they had to take over large blocks of territory if only to prevent them falling into the hands of exclusive rivals.'[2] And again, 'It was the embarkation of France, Germany and other countries on the course of Empire that brought the British to the conviction that only political control could adequately safeguard markets'.[3]

Even in the case of Germany, this explanation probably

[1] Probably the most instructive episode here is the struggle regarding China. The British were only very reluctantly converted to the principle of 'spheres of influence'. But they continually used their diplomatic machinery to press for the policy of the open door.

[2] *The Diplomacy of Imperialism*, p. 75.

[3] Ibid., p. 95. After these eminently sensible pronouncements it is something of a shock to find that, in his summing up of the whole period, at the end of the book, Professor Langer says that the Germans 'with some justice felt that John Bull, already bloated with colonial spoils, wanted the whole world *for his private preserve*' (p. 794, my italics). Private preserve is precisely the term which cannot be applied to a free trade empire. Whatever we may say about British policy in general – and the present writer has never been a silent critic of its obvious deficiencies – we must surely admit that until the introduction of the notorious Ottawa system, British trade policy was immune from the charge of sectional exclusiveness. Professor Langer goes on to say that 'it would be hopeless to try to understand the Anglo-German problem without taking account of this clash of economic forces'. It is perhaps hopeless to expect that students of diplomacy will try to understand economic theory. But before committing himself to so weighty a pronouncement, it would surely have been well for the foremost diplomatic historian of our day to have considered a little further the testimony of Prince Lichnowsky. 'England', said this candid man, 'would no more have drawn the sword against us on account of our Navy alone than she would have done so on account of our trade, which is supposed to have called forth envy and finally the war ... The theory of England's trade envy of which there has been so much talk, is based upon faulty judgment'. *Auf dem Wege zum Abgrund* I, pp. 116-118.

fits the facts more often than any other. It is true that owing to the cartel policy which was fostered by the German government, there was a contact between certain groups of German industrialists and the German government probably closer than existed in any other country; and it is possible that some at least of the German expansion was initiated in such circles — not, be it noted, the circles of high finance. It is true, moreover, that the writings of the ruling school of German economists went far to justify a policy of aggressive trade expansion. But although these had some influence at the time, it is probable that the main lines of Bismarckian policy were dictated by defensive considerations. The change in Bismarck's attitude to the colonial question coincided with the general return to protectionism, of which of course he was so largely the architect; and, taking into account what we know of the man and his conception of his mission, it is plausible to argue that the hypothesis that he was fearful of exclusion does less injustice to the facts than the hypothesis of more active aggressiveness. The aggressive economic philosophy had more influence on Bismarck's successors and on their military and naval staffs than it had on the Iron Chancellor. But for the full fruition of such teaching we have had to wait for the practice of the Third Reich. Fear of exclusion was probably the dominating motive of the earlier period.

In the years since the Great War of 1914-18, such fears have been increasingly justified. Beside the gigantic restrictionist apparatus of the 'post-war' period, the earlier tariff walls are mere pigmies. If the statesmen of the times of our fathers had reason to fear the exclusiveness of their neighbours, justification for such fears has been afforded to us in double measure. It is no accident that this age affords a classic example of an expansionist war designed to relieve such restrictions. Whatever we may think of the justice of the Japanese attack on China, there can be no doubt of its connection with the restriction of the Japanese market. In 1929, with the advent of the Great Depression, the market for Japanese silk in the United States and elsewhere collapsed. Now silk was the chief item of Japanese export. The collapse was a major catastrophe. It was only to be expected, therefore, that the Japanese would turn as rapidly as possible to other forms of export. This they did; and immediately the markets elsewhere were effectively closed against them. In Ceylon, for instance, in one year the import of a certain kind of Japanese cloth was reduced to one-tenth of its former dimensions. The connection between such events and the invasion of China is so obvious as to need no elaboration.

It is not only restrictions on trade which have become more menacing in the most recent period; there has emerged also a type of policy from which the earlier period was almost entirely free, the policy of restriction of migration. In the years before the Great War it was possible to travel from one end of Europe to the other without a passport; and the enterprising youth of the more congested areas had no difficulty in transferring their efforts to areas offering greater scope. We have changed all that nowadays. The political exile crouches in ditches between frontiers and the youth of impoverished Europe, denied access to the open spaces, dons a shirt and prepares for the wars. The present generation of Englishmen, to whom the obligation to carry a passport has rapidly become part of the natural order of things, have never paid much attention to the effects of the stoppage of migration. But there can be little doubt that, in a world perspective, it has been one of the most potent factors making for conflict. It is very difficult to take seriously the complaints of dictators who impede emigration and encourage the birth rate. But their subjects nevertheless have a real and legitimate grievance.

It would be a great mistake, however, to regard the tensions of this period as springing merely from fear of economic exclusion. Enough has been said earlier to make it clear that there is no intention here to ascribe the spiritual disease, the collective schizophrenia of Europe, to purely economic factors. But it is worth noting that, with the rise of the totalitarian systems, the aggressive economic motive has become more and more in evidence. In the Nazi literature, the desire for expansion is not merely a desire to escape the effects of other peoples' restrictions; it is much more a desire positively to exploit subject races and to dominate the world. We are no longer moving within the intellectual limits of the assumptions of nineteenth-century diplomacy. In the ideology of pre-war Europe, the exploitation of even the most backward people by non-reciprocal trade restrictions was becoming slightly discredited. In the practice of totalitarian Germany, not only is the concept of subject peoples enlarged to include, for instance, Czechs and Jews, but the admissibility of forced labour, that is the virtual restoration of slavery, is also taken more or less for granted. The economic motives of the powers who became involved in the catastrophe of the Great War of 1914-18, were the motives of distrustful and irascible but, for the most part, fairly civilized men. The economic motives of the totalitarian powers are the motives of barbarian hordes.

CHAPTER V

THE ULTIMATE CAUSE OF INTERNATIONAL CONFLICT

1 *The Final Task*

WE have now some idea of the way in which different types of economic causes — in the sense of economic motives — can lead to international conflict; and we have attempted to establish some sense of proportion concerning their relative importance in different periods. So far as the modern period is concerned, we have found reason to believe that, with the growth of national restrictionism, there existed for the different nations, genuine defensive interests going far to justify the diplomatic struggle for power.

We cannot rest here, however. Our analysis, so far, has been concerned principally with causes in the sense of motives. Before it can be regarded as in any sense complete, it is necessary to consider causes in a wider sense. It is necessary to ask whether there do not exist conditions more general than any we have so far examined, which are conducive to the appearance of these motives. Do they arise only within certain patterns of economic institutions? Are there modes of political organization which facilitate their emergence? We have not left these things altogether out of account; but we must now deal with them specifically and in greater detail.

2 *The Concomitants of 'Dollar Diplomacy'*

We may start with the type of cause which we have found to be less general than others, at any rate in recent times: Lenin's case of the pressure of investors to defend or facilitate their foreign investments. We shall find that the type of conclusion which we reach here anticipates, as it were, in a minor key, the type of conclusion which will be the main theme of the chapter. We shall find profound political factors complicating our economic analysis.

The question we have to answer is whether, when the pressure of investment capital is found to be actively influential in producing diplomatic friction, there are accompanying conditions of a more general character which can be interpreted as having causal significance. In the case of the Boer War, for instance, is there a wider setting which may be regarded as in any sense typical?

The answer is fairly simple. In nearly all such cases it will be found that there is political weakness on the capital-importing side.[1] There is weakness in the sense that the government of the capital-exporting country is prepared to take risks on behalf of its investors, which it would be reluctant to take if its opponent were stronger. There is weakness, too, in the sense that the types of commercial law in vogue in the capital-importing country and the standards of its administration are different from those obtaining in the areas of fully developed western civilization. This is a point which is often elided by the chivalrous critics of this kind of imperialism. But on an objective view there can be no doubt that, judged by western standards, the appeals of traders and investors for protection against arbitrary confiscation, discriminating justice and administrative corruption, have often had much justification. Trade between states with western standards of justice and administration, be they weak or

[1] This is a branch of the subject which Mr. Staley has made his own. See his *War and the Private Investor*, especially chapters 13 and 14.

strong, in the military sense, does not involve 'protection' to nationals. As Mr. Lippmann has well remarked, 'You do not have to wrap the flag round trade in regions where a fairly modern government exists'.[1] I myself think that the Boer War was a stain on our national record. But I do not see how any candid man can deny great provocation on the part of the Kruger government. Only those who hold that sovereign states have, not merely the power, but the right to do anything they like within their own borders, can regard such cases as involving only simple moral issues. For those who look upon state sovereignty as being, with all other human institutions, subject to the dictates of general social utility, the problem is much more difficult. But, be this as it may, we may regard it as established that a predisposing condition to the operation of this kind of economic cause is a certain disharmony of political arrangements.

3 *The Causes of Economic Nationalism*

As we have seen, however, this type of case is exceptional, at any rate in the 'most recent period of capitalism'. As we have seen, the main cause has been the fear of exclusion from economic opportunities in other territories. The *raison d'être* of the struggle for national power, in so far as it is economic in origin, is fear of other nations' restriction. We have seen that the interest here defended can legitimately be regarded as an interest of the majority of the citizens. But we have not yet inquired concerning the nature of the interests underlying the restrictions against which national interests are defended or the nature of the institutions under which such interests emerge. To do this is the main task of this chapter.

Now of course it would be an exaggeration to attribute

---

[1] *The Stakes of Diplomacy*, p. 166.

all restrictions on trade to the pressure of sinister interest. Restrictions have sometimes been imposed for military reasons; a sacrifice of other real income has been thought worth while for the gain in security. There are sometimes sinister interests involved here. The groups of producers who gain may succeed in exaggerating the importance and necessity of their contribution to national safety; British sugar-beet growers have long battened on policies which have been the product of this sort of propaganda. But this need not be the case. Given the prospect of war, many measures, which otherwise would be wholly pernicious, may be claimed to be in the national interest. This is a case where Mr. Hawtrey's dictum that the chief cause of war is war itself receives interesting exemplification.

Apart from this, however, there are occasions when restrictions may appear to serve the national interest in the strictly economic sense. We need not waste time here examining the list of exceptional cases (worked out by the theorists of free trade) where it is conceivable that, in the long run, carefully devised restrictions might secure some gain — the so-called 'terms of trade' case, etc. These are intellectual *curiosa* which can only be used for justifying the actual measures imposed in the rough and tumble of everyday politics, by the ignorant or the interested.[1] But, at times of trade depression when employment is slack, the imposition of restrictions may appear to have a more obvious advantage — the advantage of reducing unemployment in particular lines of industry. It is clear that these advantages disappear in the long run. It is clear that, even in the short run, restrictive measures provoke retaliations and dislocations

[1] For a more extensive treatment of these matters see my *Economic Planning and International Order*.

which go far to wipe out even the transitory gains which such measures may appear to promise. It is clear that, if new measures of this sort are imposed in every new depression, the 'cure' of unemployment thus achieved is likely to be much worse than the disease. But it is an important fact that the situation at the bottom of a trade depression produces an atmosphere peculiarly favourable to protectionist propaganda; historically many upward changes in tariffs have come about at these times.

This, indeed, is the sediment of truth in the underconsumptionist theories of imperialism. The theoretical analysis on which they have been based has usually been faulty. As we have seen, when they are phrased in terms which are free from analytical error, they do not prove their main contention. It is doubtful, too, whether even those forms which are freest from logical error correctly describe the majority of actual trade cycles. But it is a fact that the fear of recurrent depression and the accompanying shrinkage of spending does play a powerful part in predisposing the public at large to accept measures which otherwise it might more actively resent. If the trade cycle could be eliminated, the propagandist case for restriction would be very substantially weakened.

In spite of this, it is to lose all sense of proportion to describe the trade cycle, whatever its origin, as the main cause of restrictionism. The main cause of restrictionism is the pressure of sinister interest, a pressure which is active both in periods of good trade and of bad. It is no accident that, speaking broadly, over the last seventy years the extent of restrictionism in various countries has varied with the susceptibility of governments to the pressure of private interests. Where the susceptibility of governments to this kind of pressure has been great, there restrictionism has been rampant. Where public opinion has been better informed and where standards of politics and administration have been high, there restrictionism has been relatively mild. It is notorious that, in many parts of the world, public opinion has not been very well informed and governmental standards have not been high.

Here, at last then, we find a place in our main theory for the influence of sinister interests — interests, that is to say, which are not the interests of the national group as a whole. These interests do not usually produce conflict directly. It is the exception rather than the rule for governments to risk serious diplomatic friction in the interests of an economic group. The immediate cause of conflict is the desire of governments to maintain or extend their power — a national not a sinister interest. The ulterior purpose here is the safeguarding of the economic opportunities of the citizens — again a national not a sinister interest. But this aim would not arise were it not for the practices of restrictionism; and these practices must be ascribed in large part to the influence of pressure groups. Thus our theory leaves ample scope for the play of disinterested public spirit and genuine intellectual error. It does not attribute to the pressure groups any conscious desire to cause diplomatic complications. It does not suggest that the executives of the manufacturers' associations or trade unions who lobby for restrictionist legislation, ever dream that their actions will provide other governments with a justification for policies which may lead to war. But it argues that, nevertheless, through the indirect mechanisms described, war may be the eventual outcome. Such an analysis is surely more in harmony with our everyday experience of human action, with its mixed motives, its shortsightedness, and its muddles, than the penny-dreadful type of explanation which sees ruthless and machiavellian economic interest behind every incident of diplomatic friction.

At the same time it must be noticed that the sectional interests invoked by our theory are not usually the interests contemplated by the Marxians. The interests which we find to be active are not class interests in the Marxian sense, they are sectional interests having common prospects of monopoly gains in the market.

Thus, if we take the influence of property owners, it is at once obvious that it is not property owners as a class who are active; it is particular groups of property owners, who hope that the value of their special kind of property will be enhanced by the limitation of markets. There is no reason at all to suppose that the whole class of property owners actually gains by the practices of trade restriction. Some groups of property owners gain, others lose; and, on balance, there is probably net loss. Nor is there any evidence that property owners as a class show any solidarity here. The pressure groups whose operation can actually be observed are not constituted on a 'horizontal' basis at all. Their constitution is essentially 'vertical'. It is particular industries and trades with obviously homogeneous market interests which are the breeding ground of restrictionist pressure.

Moreover, this kind of interest is not limited to groups of property owners. If the movement of labour between industrial groups were completely free, then, in the long run, the workers in any branch would have no particular interest in restriction; only the owners of more specific factors could ultimately hope to benefit. But in fact the movement of labour is not free; and to obtain the limitation of markets is sometimes as much an interest of the workers as it is of the capitalists. We see this clearly enough when particular measures of protectionism are under debate in political assemblies. It is notorious that, in such countries as the United States of America and Australia, groups of trade unionists have been at least as zealous as groups of capitalists in promoting measures of trade restriction. In Great Britain, where the free trade tradition was strongly rooted on the left, this kind of thing was very infrequent until a short time ago. But now that free trade practice has gone by the board, we have already witnessed the alliance of particular groups of capital and labour to obtain sectional privilege; and, as time goes on, this kind of alignment is likely to become more frequent. To argue that interest in restrictions is confined essentially to property owners is out of harmony both with theory and with the facts.

We can see this all the more clearly if we turn for a moment to the other relevant type of restriction, restrictions on immigration.

As we have seen, at the present day such restrictions are among the chief causes of international tension. But no one with any sense of reality could ascribe them to the influence of groups of property owners. The interests of property owners in general are indeed quite obviously opposed to restrictions on immigration; and it is notorious that, both in Australia and in the United States, it has been the influence of trade unions which has been predominant in securing their imposition. It is perhaps doubtful whether the long-run interests of the labouring classes as a whole are as opposed to immigration as is often supposed. The economics of migration in a *milieu* of declining population are highly complicated; and a good case could be made out for the view that, on balance, the majority of the working classes in many national areas would be gainers from such a movement. But the interests of particular groups are obviously directly endangered and their influence accordingly has been all in favour of restriction. A more complete justification for the desire to maintain and extend the area of national sovereignty is scarcely possible to imagine. But it certainly cannot be described as emanating from capitalist sources.

The Marxians were right in suspecting that in the causation of major wars there was sinister interest operating somewhere. But they mistook the nature of the interest. It is not the interests of the capitalists as a class, but the interests of sectional groups (who may be groups of capitalists or groups of workers or temporary alliances of both) which give rise to the practices of restrictionism which are indirectly responsible for war.

4 *The Wars of a National Socialist World*

It is possible that all this might be granted and that yet it might be argued that the very existence of sectional interest in this sense is only possible under capitalism. Sweep away production for profit, it might be said, nationalize the means of production, and the disharmonies which have been diagnosed under capitalism, will automatically disappear.

This belief is general among socialists. Eager to build socialist institutions within the framework of the sovereign states within which they happen to be living, it seldom if ever occurs to them to ask whether the achievement of socialism within national units is compatible with the ultimate achievement of the international socialism to which most of them give lip service.[1] Yet the ownership and control of the means of production by the different

---

[1] There are of course exceptions, from Trotsky to Bertrand Russell. But it is not unfair to add that, by the majority of active socialist politicians such exceptions are regarded as cranks.

geographical groups which are the present sovereign states, is palpably not the same as the ownership of the means of production by the citizens of the world; and, in fact, there is strong reason to believe that national collectivism is likely to create international disharmonies at once more glaring and more dangerous than any which arise under capitalism. The bellicosity of the national socialism of Germany and Italy is certainly due to many factors other than economic. But it is not altogether an accident. There are inherent in the fundamental principles of national collectivism certain basic assumptions which make conflict with other national units almost inevitable.

Let us take for a moment a hypothetical example, free from the disagreeable and tendentious associations of European national politics. Let us suppose, what is not altogether improbable, that in the course of the next few years, the economic system of Australia or New Zealand becomes completely collectivist. The inhabitants of these areas are not Nazis. They inherit much of the easy-going and friendly traditions of British politics in general. It is most improbable, within any time about which it is worth while speculating, that they would be inspired by motives of external aggressiveness. Yet, unless they were desperately in need of man power for military purposes or unless they were threatened with extreme depopulation, it is not to be expected that they would be any more willing than they have been in the recent past to admit immigration on a large scale. On the contrary, there is every reason to suppose that the incentive to oppose such a policy would be even stronger than before. Under capitalism, the incentive is concern with the level of labour incomes only. Under national socialism it is concern with incomes per head from all sources. Under national socialism, the workers are interested, not only in the level of wages but also in the level of rents; and while more labour would raise the marginal productivity of land, there would come a point at which additional claimants on the total of rents would mean less per head to go round.

Now suppose that, simultaneously with these developments in richer areas, national socialism is also instituted in areas less well provided. The inhabitants of such areas would have no further hope of improving their position by appropriating the rents of internal property owners, for by hypothesis, these rents would already have been appropriated. They would have little hope of migrating to areas more richly endowed, for the inhabitants of such areas would cling tenaciously to their rents. In such circumstances would there not be solid justification for envy? Would there not be a standing justification for attempts to enlarge the national boundaries, for attempts to secure a *Lebensraum* more richly endowed with the material factors of production?

But, if this were so, then the struggle for power would be perpetuated. The inhabitants of the richer states would have to be prepared to defend attacks on their possessions. They would have to maintain military and naval forces and to safeguard their position by suitable alliances. Attempts might be made to secure 'international understanding'. Leagues of nations might be proposed and, in intervals between times of tension, might flourish for a while. But, while the inequality of possessions persisted and while the inhabitants of the richer areas, maintaining national independence, refused to share their higher incomes with the inhabitants of the poorer areas, it would all be a fool's paradise. Underneath, the basic disharmony would persist; and only power and accident would keep the peace.

Our example is, of course, conjectural; and always in conjectural examples there is the possibility that some element which may have an important modifying influence has been overlooked. But our picture is not so unlike contemporary reality as to warrant much hope that the model is very misleading. We do not find, in the poorer areas of national collectivism, any strong disposition to be content with a position of inferiority. Nor do we find in the richer areas, any disposition to forgo either the gains of monopoly or the advantages of restrictions on migration. Before the invasion of Poland it used to be said that the policy of Soviet Russia was consistently non-aggressive. But this was merely a particularly significant example of the incapacity of English intellectuals to see straight where Russia is concerned. Revolutionary Russia showed no scruple in invading Georgia; and the socialization of the apparatus of production of Russian urban industry did not prevent the invasion of the rural areas and the appropriation of kulak rents. Rosa Luxemburg's book is full of complaints of the destruction of peasant economy by capitalist exploiters. But it is doubtful whether there is any example in history of the destruction of a peasant economy more ruthless or more complete than the destruction of the Russian peasantry under Stalin's first five year plan.

The fact is that, once states take over, on an extensive scale, the ownership of the material factors of production within their borders,[1] the distinction between territorial jurisdiction and property disappears and, *for that very reason*, the fact of geographical inequality becomes a permanent cause of disharmony. Under liberalism there

[1] It is not denied that governments must necessarily own certain types of productive factors, such as roads, which are characterized in one way or another by extensive indivisibility. But this is quite different from general ownership of mines, land and the apparatus of manufacture.

is inevitably some inequality of private property; and this, as we know, is apt to breed envy and disunity. But the inequality of atomistic private property is something much less permanent, much less intractable than the inequality of state possessions. The one is something which is continually changing with the passing of successive generations, and which is susceptible of profound modification by taxation and changes in the law of inheritance. The other is something which is as permanent as the states themselves, and which is only capable of modification by force or the threat of force. A world of national socialist states is analytically on all fours with the world of primitive times when the rival hordes owned and had 'sovereignty' over the lands over which they roved, and when the existence of rich soils, good hunting grounds and accumulated treasure, side by side with poor soils, lean hunting grounds and inferior accumulations, was a standing cause of brutal and total war.[1]

International liberals and international socialists can surely be at one in this conclusion, that national ownership of the means of production is not conducive either to international union or to international peace. There is no reason to suppose that the coming of national socialism all round would diminish the economic causes of war.

5 *The Root Cause of International Conflict*

If this is true, there follows a conclusion, the importance of which for the correct understanding of the ultimate

---

[1] In his book on the national problem, Otto Bauer, the well-known leader of the Austrian Socialists, actually points out that national socialism involves the national state as rent receiver and the limitation of migration: *Die Nationalitäten Frage und der Sozialdemokratie*, p. 515. But, inexplicably, he then assumes that such disharmonies would be peaceably adjusted and that the society of the future would be 'ein bunter Bild von nationalen personen Verbänden'. There seems no reason whatever to suppose that such would in fact be the case.

causes of war it is almost impossible to exaggerate. The ultimate condition giving rise to those clashes of national economic interest which lead to international war is the existence of independent national sovereignties. Not capitalism, but the anarchic political organization of the world is the root disease of our civilization.

Against this, however, it might be argued that such conflicts are not necessary. If the different sovereign states would abstain from the practices of restrictionism, if their citizens would banish from their hearts the desire for sectional advantage, these things need not happen. Rightly interpreted, the long-run interests of the inhabitants of the different national areas are not in disharmony. Whatever the prospects of momentary advantage from restrictionist manipulation and aggression, in the modern world at least, the long-run interests of all who are not sadistic maniacs lie above all in the preservation of peace.

Such was the belief of the Cobdenite liberals, in spite of the jeers of the uneducated, probably the most disinterested body of men who ever influenced the policy of a great nation. But, in spite of its nobility, it was grounded in error. It is true that, rightly interpreted, the long-run interests of the majority of the human race are not in conflict. It is true that, for humane men, the disaster of war is an evil of the first order of magnitude. But it is not true that, in the absence of the rule of law, there is any security against its occurrence. The Cobdenite liberals would have never dreamt of urging that, within national areas, the long-run interests of the majority in peaceful co-operation could be regarded as secured without a framework of law and coercion. Such a view would have been the view, not of liberals, but of philosophical anarchists. What justification had they, therefore, for assuming that, in the relations between the inhabitants of different national areas, a superior harmony might be expected? If they did not expect the mere demonstration of long-run interest, unsupported by law, to secure an absence of anti-social behaviour *within* the nation, why should they have expected that it would do so *between* nations, where the play of irrational prejudice and the lack of understanding and sympathy were so much more likely to be prevalent?[1] Surely the truth is that, if the different national governments are free to do anything, there is a strong probability that, with the best will in the world on the part of the majority, from time to time, error or sinister interest will result in policies leading to disharmony.

We can see this very plainly if we turn for a moment from the relations of geographical groups to the relations of groups of producers. It is possible to argue that, rightly interpreted, the interests of different groups of producers are not in long-period disharmony. If one group alone restricts output, it is quite possible that it may gain; but if all groups play the same game, then most at least will be the poorer. Nevertheless, knowledge of such long-period

[1] I cannot help thinking that my friend, Mr. E. L. Woodward, makes just the wrong point against Cobdenism when (in his interesting essay on *War and Peace in Europe* 1815-1870) he asks would such thinkers have been willing to 'apply, as between state and state, forms of co-operation and mutual aid which they rejected in a sphere more directly under their control'? (p. 71). So far as the sphere directly under the control of the national states was concerned, no Cobdenite ever thought of rejecting the co-ordinating aid of the framework of law and order. If they had been willing to see established, between state and state, the form of organization which they supported within states, the international anarchy would have disappeared. Support of a policy of permitting, within a co-ordinating framework of law, the free movement of capital and labour, is not support of a policy permitting sovereign individuals to do exactly as they please; and there would have been no inconsistency in demanding an apparatus of international co-ordination and coercion, while holding that, within such a framework, the common interest might best be served by a system of decentralized initiative resting on private property and the market.

harmonies does not justify us in believing that, if groups of producers are given by statute a position of uncontrolled monopolistic privilege, the prospect of short-period gain will not tempt them very often to abuse it. It is true that governments have sometimes acted on this assumption and that the 'experts' they have consulted have done nothing to warn them of its dangers. But experience shows that it is unwarranted. If groups of producers are given positions of monopolistic privilege, a state of affairs is created in which the emergence of policies tending to disharmony can be regarded as almost inevitable.

In exactly the same way, if geographical groups have uncontrolled powers of restriction and exclusion, if there is no framework of law limiting the actions of independent sovereign states, then a state of affairs exists in which the abuse of these powers is probable. There exists a state of affairs in which the delusions of restrictionism and the sinister influence of the pressure groups have maximum scope and effectiveness — a state of affairs in which the deep-seated non-rational impulses of nationalism have the maximum opportunity to become entangled in the support of economic policies which ultimately lead to war. However true it may be that, in the long run, such policies can be shown to lead to impoverishment and international conflict, there is no reason to suppose that, in the absence of the restraints of a rule of law, the majority of the citizens will be sufficiently alert or sufficiently long sighted to prevent their emergence. A world organization which depends upon the continual dominance in every sovereign state of the principles of Cobdenite liberalism, is an organization which is bound not infrequently to be disorganized. The dominance in one important state or group of states of different principles is liable to endanger the whole system. A system of sovereign geographical groups is no less likely to be provocative of clashes of interest than a system of 'sovereign' groups of producers.

All this becomes very clear if we take a hypothetical example, which, but for the foresight of a small group of men and the courage and consistency of their successors, might easily have become an example in actual history.

Under the constitution of the United States of America, the governments of the different states are prohibited from imposing protective tariffs on imports or exports. They are prohibited from limiting migration or the movement of capital. All these matters are the prerogative of the federal government.

Let us suppose that things had been different. Suppose that the Constitutional Congress had broken down and there had eventually arisen, in that great area, instead of one federation, forty-eight independent sovereign states.

Does any man of experience doubt for a moment that there would have arisen also, in America as in Europe, a network of restriction on interstate economic relations? Trade would have been limited. The interests in various states would have protested against the 'flood of cheap imports'; even under the present constitution there are formidable barriers in the shape of spurious veterinary regulations and such-like measures not guarded against by the founders of the constitution.[1] Migration would have been hampered. If prosperity in one part was greater than in another, there would have been protests against the 'flood of immigrant labour'; in the recent depression, unconstitutional limitations of this sort have actually been attempted by various states. Relations of debtors and creditors would have been endangered. If the states of the middle west were depressed, not only would there be

[1] For a good account of these see RAYMOND BUELL, *Death by Tariff*, Chicago University Press.

isolated failures to keep faith with eastern creditors, there would also be imposed the paralysing apparatus of exchange control and partial repudiation with which European practice has made us familiar. And the result of all this would be interstate conflict. The different governments would feel it incumbent on them to maintain national power by alliances and manœuvres. The inhabitants of the poorer states would covet the privileges of the richer states. There would be talk of the necessity for *Lebensraum*. Where debt was repudiated, the cause of the investors might become a matter of diplomatic friction; it is easy to imagine an expeditionary force from New York invading, let us say, Kansas to protect the interests of the bond-holders.

In short, we should be confronted with the whole dreary spectacle of power politics with its manœuvres, its devotions, its mass sentiment, and its background of sinister interest, with which the history of unhappy Europe has made us so depressingly familiar. And the pacifists would say that it was due to lack of virtue. The biologists would say it was an aspect of the inevitable struggle for existence. The psychologists would say it was a manifestation of the death instinct which it would take a thousand years research to learn to sublimate.[1] The Marxians would say it was all due to the capitalist system. And certain among the historians would hint that it was the result of dark subtle forces of which only they understood the mystery.

But in fact, it would be due to the existence of independent sovereign states. No doubt it would be possible to

---

[1] See e.g. Dr. E. R. GLOVER'S *War, Pacifism and Sadism* – a good example of the way in which one of the profoundest discoveries of our age can be made ridiculous by superficial application. It is interesting to compare Dr. Glover's wearying *épatism* with the restraint and insight of Freud. See especially *Civilization, War and Death passim.*

investigate further the catastrophe which had brought it about that this, rather than federation, had been the line of evolution. If Hamilton had not lived or if Lincoln had faltered . . . . or if the economic interests of dissenting states had succeeded in securing the rejection of the proposals of the Constitutional Congress — any of these things might have caused the path of history to be different. But in the sense in which cause may be said to be a condition in the absence of which subsequent events could not have happened, the existence of independent sovereign states ought be justly regarded as the fundamental cause of conflict. And since we know that it was deliberately to avoid such a state of chaos that Hamilton and his friends devised the existing constitution, we may well regard their motives as the cause of its freedom from this kind of embarrassment. In the sense which is significant for political action, it is the chaos of independent sovereignties which is the ultimate condition of international conflict. It is not only because the independent states have the power to declare war, that war is sometimes declared, it is also because they have the power to adopt policies involving clashes of national interest of which war seems the only solution.

6 *The United States of Europe*

If this is so, then the remedy is plain. Independent sovereignty must be limited. As citizens of the various national states, we may hope to diminish the danger of conflict by opposing policies which tend to evoke it. But this is not enough. The apparatus of modern war is so formidable, the cost of its maintenance so onerous, the dangers of actual conflict are so great, that we cannot afford to rely on spontaneous goodwill as our only safeguard against catastrophe. There must be an international framework of law and order, supported by solid sanctions which prevent the emergence of those policies which are eventually responsible for conflict. We do not need a unitary world state; such an organization would be neither practicable nor desirable. But we do need a federal organization; not a mere confederation of sovereign states as was the League of Nations, but a genuine federation which takes over from the states of which it is composed, those powers which engender conflict. The founders of the League of Nations were right in that they recognized the need of a supernational authority; their error was that they did not go far enough. They did not realize that the effective functioning of a supernational authority is incompatible with independent national sovereignty. But to-day we know this. The history of the League of Nations is one long demonstration of the truth of the proposition long ago set forth by Hamilton and Madison, that there is no safety in confederations. We know to-day that unless we destroy the sovereign state, the sovereign state will destroy us.[1]

Now, of course, it is quite Utopian to hope for the formation in our time of a federation of world dimensions. There is not sufficient feeling of a common citizenship. There is as yet no sufficiently generalized culture. In present conditions, even the electoral problems of such a body would present insurmountable difficulties. The formation of a world system, the political consummation of the unity of the human race, may well be regarded as the divine event towards which all that is good in the heritage of the diverse civilizations of the world, invites us to strive. But, whatever we may hope for in the distant

[1] For a fuller elaboration of these arguments see my *Economic Planning and International Order*, chaps. ix, x and xi. The general argument of MR. CLARENCE STREIT's *Union Now* should also be consulted.

future of the planet, it must be clear that, at the present stage of human development, any attempt at so comprehensive an organization would be necessarily doomed to disaster.

But it is not Utopian to hope for the construction of more limited federations — for the merging of independent sovereignties in areas where there exists the consciousness of a common civilization and a need for greater unity. In particular it is not Utopian to hope for the formation of a structure of this kind in that part of the world now most menaced by the contradictions of its present political organization — among the warring sovereignties of Europe.[1] So far is it from being Utopian that, for those with eyes to see, it is the most urgent practical necessity of the age.

For it is surely plain that the present political organization of Europe has completely outlived its usefulness and is now nothing but a menace to the very existence of the civilization it has helped to bring forth. When the sovereign states of modern Europe emerged from the feudalism of

---

[1] Perhaps a word is necessary here concerning the relation of the suggestion here put forward and that put forward by Mr. C. K. Streit. Mr. Streit's scheme, it will be remembered, is for a union of the Atlantic democracies including the United States and the British Empire. I have no objection to this. If Mr. Streit could induce his fellow-countrymen to come forward with the proposal, I should be delighted to see our government accept it; the larger the federation, the smaller the area of future wars. But I think it very unlikely that this will happen. It does not seem probable that, in our generation at least, the citizens of the United States will feel that compelling urge to union with other peoples which would alone make it possible. On the other hand, the disunity of Europe is so great and the evils likely to result from its persistence are so frightful, that it seems possible that, out of the extremity of our danger, a movement for unity might arise. After all there is a common European consciousness; and it is surely in the logic of history that sooner or later this should be enshrined in common political institutions. I see no insurmountable difficulty in the relation of the British Dominions to a federal Europe. Either they could enter the federation as full members; or they could retain via the British Crown the same loose relation as exists at present. I see much greater difficulty in the inclusion of Russia. For Russia is not European in spirit; and totalitarian dictatorship is incompatible with the federation of free peoples.

the middle ages, their functions were liberalizing and creative. They eliminated the mass of local restrictions which were strangling economic development. They pacified the warring barons and princes and established uniformity of law over areas given over to particularism. But, at the present time, it is, not their unifying, but their separatist tendencies which have become dominant. They restrict the activities of an economic life which, in its spontaneous development, spreads far beyond their borders. They are uneconomic units for the administration of what positive functions they discharge; and the burden of maintaining the apparatus of defence which is necessary to secure their independence, threatens more and more to absorb all the energies of their inhabitants. The existence of restrictions to trade and movement between the different states of Europe to-day is as absurd as the existence of similar restrictions between different provinces at earlier periods. To an intelligent outsider unacquainted with the background of our history, the maintenance of vast armies by the states of Europe for defence against each other must be hardly less ridiculous than would be the maintenance of armies for the separate defence of the towns or departments within these states. The system has reached breaking point; and, with the development of modern military techniques, it has no longer survival value. As gunpowder rendered obsolete the feudal system, so the aeroplane renders obsolete the system of the independent sovereignties of Europe. A more comprehensive type of organization is inevitable. Will it come by mutual agreement or by caesarian conquest? That is the unsolved question. For either there must be empire or federation; on a long view, there is no alternative.

But to create such a federation will not be easy. We have a common culture. But we have no common language.

We have a common history. But it is riven by fratricidal quarrels. No one who has realized the nature of the interests involved in the perpetuation of the present powers of the independent sovereign states can be blind to the strength of the opposition to any attempt to eliminate our disunity. The federation of the thirteen secession states of the new world was almost wrecked by local particularism, even though they were united by a common tongue, common habits and the memory of recent action against a common enemy. How much harder must it be for the warring states of Europe, with none of these aids, to establish a basis of unity. It will not be easy to make the new Europe.

Nevertheless, of all the tasks which present themselves to our generation, it is that which is most worth while attempting. The age in which we live is an age in which men have worshipped many idols and followed many false visions. It has seen nationalism run mad and collectivism turn oppressor. The ideals of the romantic rebellion have proved dead sea fruit in our hands. But the great ideals of liberty, justice and mutual tolerance and the heritage of art and learning which is their spiritual outcome, have not been found wanting. The more they have become endangered, the more important we have discovered them to be. But it is just these things which are in peril from the disunity of Europe. The political structure amid which they have developed has developed stresses and strains which threaten to overwhelm them; if they are to be preserved, a constructive effort is necessary. Not merely because war is terrible, not merely because it impoverishes, but because it threatens all that is most valuable in the cultural heritage of Europe, we must devise institutions which banish it from our midst. It is because the civilization of Socrates and Spinoza, of Shakespeare and Beethoven, of Michelangelo and Rembrandt, of Newton and Pascal, is at stake that we must build a new Europe.

And now that the war has come and our hopes of peaceful developments lie shattered, this necessity is all the greater if the end is not to be chaos. We are fighting Germans. If European civilization is not to perish, we must destroy the tyranny which rules over them. No one with any sense of history and art will deny the existence of a real German problem in Europe — the incapacity for self-government, the tendency to brutality and sadism, the fascination with the death motive, the moral clumsiness, the deep sense of spiritual insecurity, which again and again, since the rise of Prussia, have been a menace to the peace and liberties of Europe. But for all that, Germans are Europeans. They are part of our civilization; and Europe can never be completely healthy till Germany is healthy too. Somehow or other we must create a framework in which the German *Geist* can give its best, not its worst, to Europe. A draconian peace will do nothing. The Nazis must be extirpated; but we have neither the strength nor the will to keep Germans in subjection for ever. What more appropriate outcome of our present agonies, therefore, what more fitting consecration of the blood which is being shed, than a peace in which this great people, purged of its devils, shall be coerced into free and equal citizenship of the United States of Europe?

THE MEANING OF ECONOMIC CAUSATION

1 *Introduction*

THE purpose of this appendix is to make precise some of the notions used in the foregoing chapters, in particular the concept of economic causation. When we say that a certain war was due to economic causes what exactly do we mean? What must be the nature of any general theory of the economic causes of war? The inquiry may seem to be unnecessarily abstract. But in view of the extraordinary ambiguity of everyday language in this connection a short clarification of our ideas is perhaps not without its uses.

2 *The Notion of an Historical Cause*

Before doing this, however, there are certain points concerning historical explanations of any kind to which it is desirable to draw attention.

To say that one event is due to another is always a very hazardous procedure. For, strictly speaking, it is possible to argue that anything that happens anywhere at any moment is a resultant of what has happened everywhere at every preceding moment. To explain exhaustively the history of anything involves retailing exhaustively the history of everything. There is no such thing as isolated causation.

In spite of this, in everyday life, we do not feel under such encyclopaedic obligations; and, even in serious historical explanation, our objective is much more limited. For, while it would be wrong to pick out any single antecedent of any given event and claim that it was the *sole* cause of that event, it does not seem absurd to single out certain particular antecedents and to regard them as the *significant* causes. Significant causes in this sense are those antecedents in whose absence the event to be explained would obviously have been different; and they are singled out from other antecedents which it is easy to conceive changed without any obvious effect on the incident under examination. Thus, if the Prussians had not arrived on the field of Waterloo at a certain critical moment, it is probable that the whole outcome of the battle would have been different. In this sense we can regard their arrival as a significant cause of the allied victory. That they were commanded by Blücher, rather than by some other general of good military intelligence, is a fact which does not seem to have the same importance.

Now, with some events, it is what happens just before which appears to have this critical significance. Let us suppose, for instance, an international crisis which is in course of being settled peaceably. Let us suppose that, by some mistake of a wireless operator, a message which was intended to run 'Don't commence hostilities' is delivered with the 'don't' omitted. In such a case we should be justified in regarding the mistake as a significant cause of the fighting which followed. We could, of course, go back into the causes of the operator's conduct, the stresses of a long period of duty, his relations with his wife or his parents . . . and for certain purposes this would be a legitimate extension of the inquiry. But, for most purposes, explanation of the causes of the fighting would be completed by the discovery of his mistake.

Unfortunately most historical events are not capable of such easy explanation. Very often the immediate antecedents of an event seem very unimportant compared with others more remote in time. Wide tendencies discernible in the middle distance may make the *minutiae* of the immediate foreground seem relatively insignificant. In the history of the causes of the Great War of 1914-18, for instance, it is customary to argue that the details of the comings and goings of the last few weeks before the final outbreak were of small account compared with the history of the broad diplomatic groupings and ambitions which seemed to make such a catastrophe sooner or later almost inevitable. We attach more importance to the Drang nach Osten than to the shooting of the Archduke at Sarajevo.

There are very great dangers in these broader interpretations. It is very easy to say that such and such a set of influences made such and such an outcome 'almost inevitable'. But one can never be quite sure. Suppose, for instance, that the Archduke had not been shot. Is it quite certain that there would have been a European war? Is it not conceivable that the unstable situation which then obtained might have persisted until some other 'accident' — a shift of political parties in Germany, a reshuffle of the diplomatic corps in Russia — produced a *détente* in which our history might have taken another and perhaps a happier direction?

Nevertheless, we need not make this a pretext for complete scepticism regarding remoter influences. We may agree that their operation may be deflected by subsequent developments. But if they are of such a nature as seems likely to produce a certain effect, and if that effect actually occurs, the fact that it need not have occurred should not deter us from labelling them as significant causes and giving them due weight in any general description of the incident. It is not repugnant to common sense to say that one of the causes of the American War of Independence was the commercial policy of the English government even though special incidents were needed to set the tinder alight. It is in this sense of general influences tending toward international friction and conflict that we speak of economic causes of war.

3 Motives as Causes

The difficulties which arise from the existence of proximate and remote causes are difficulties which affect any kind of explanation, whether of natural events or of human conduct. There are further difficulties, however, which arise only where human conduct is involved.

If we are explaining some event of a purely physical nature, say the release of an avalanche or the discharge of lightning, when we speak of a cause, we always refer to an antecedent event also physical in nature. The chain of explanation is homogeneous.

But, if we are explaining events in which the conduct of human beings is involved, the word cause can be used in two different senses.

We can say the cause of the American War of Independence was the desire of the Americans to be rid of an irksome regulation. Or we can say it was the landing of tea at Boston. In the one case we are referring to a motive, in the other case to an event in the outside world which (inter alia) gave rise to that motive. In the one case a reason is the cause, in the other case an external event.[1]

The two modes of explanation are not in the least incompatible. Indeed, on the assumption that human action

[1] In his illuminating work on the subject matter of the social sciences, Dr. Schütz has made much the same point with his distinction between the 'weil' and the 'um-zu-' motiv. Alfred Schütz Der Sinnhafte Aufbau der Sozialen Welt, especially pp. 93-105. See also BODE and STONIER, A New Contribution to the Methodology of the Social Sciences, 'Economica', 1937, pp. 406-424.

is influenced by psychological factors, either conscious or unconscious, both are necessary. You cannot leave out one or the other without making nonsense of history. The naive behaviourists who believe that all human behaviour can be explained in terms of successive rearrangements of organic matter could not succeed in writing one page of history in such terms.

In the last analysis, however, there is a sense in which the reason is logically prior to the occasion. For the occasion will have different results according to its interpretation and the system of motives which it evokes. If the Americans had not resented the commercial policy of the English, the landing of tea at Boston would have occasioned no international friction. Hence historical knowledge in its fullest development, while necessarily a chronicle of events, is essentially an explanation of reasons. Individual reasons may themselves prove to tend to be associated with particular social or material conditions. (There will be more to be said about that later on.) But the immediate preoccupation of historical explanation, as distinct from general sociology, is essentially the discovery of reasons. Every social event is due to the action of some individual or group of individuals. Every individual action is due to some motive, conscious or unconscious.

4 *The Nature of an Economic Cause*

It is now appropriate to approach our central problem. What is it which entitles us to refer to a particular motive as being economic in character? What is an economic cause?

At first sight the problem is simple. We all speak of economic causes; and if we make allowances for the necessary (and desirable) looseness of unpedantic speech, it is probable that we often succeed in talking sense. It is to be hoped that the subject matter of this book is not radically different from the expectations aroused by its title. Nevertheless, there are certain difficulties arising from the somewhat elusive nature of the concept of the economic, which it is desirable to resolve, if our ideas are to be at all precise.

It should be fairly clear that we cannot classify wars as economic or non-economic in origin according as they involve or do not involve economic factors of any kind. For all wars involve economic factors. All wars involve the disposition of limited resources, the counting of costs, the comparison of different objectives. It is not true that a war of religion is indifferent to economic considerations and a war for trade is determined by them. The attaining of either objective necessarily has an economic aspect.

On the other hand, if we turn from considerations of means to the realm of ultimate objectives, we are confronted with the difficulty that, in that sphere, there is nothing which can be described as economic. Every attempt to classify the ends of human activity as economic or non-economic has come to grief in the most obvious confusions. It has been said, for instance, that they are economic or non-economic according as they are material or immaterial. But to obtain shelter — a 'material' end *par excellence* — may involve no economic problem; while to obtain the delights of architectural beauty — an 'immaterial' end — may raise the economic problem in its acutest form. Again it has been said that ends are economic or non-economic according as they are self-regarding or otherwise. But to satisfy oneself may be much less of an economic problem than to secure the satisfaction of others. The fact is that there are no economic ends as such; there are only economic problems involved in the achievements of ends; and these economic problems arise, not because of the nature of the ends, but because of the limitations of the means for securing them.[1]

At first sight therefore there might seem to be a complete *impasse*. The waging of any kind of war involves economic considerations. There is no kind of ultimate end which can be called economic. Are we to conclude, then, that the search for economic motives is useless?[2]

Clearly this would be absurd; we certainly mean something when we talk of such things. And fortunately, if we look a little further, it is not difficult to find a way out. If, in everyday speech, we say that a man's motive in doing a certain thing is wholly economic, what we really mean is simply that *he regards it only as a way of securing means for satisfying his ends in general*. If he does it with only one end in mind, we do not regard his motive as economic; we regard it as having the character of the end to which it is specific. But if he does it with the desire to increase his power to satisfy ends in general, then we do regard it as economic; and we say that his action has an economic cause.

This way of speaking has its counterpart in the more technical regions of economic analysis. Rightly conceived, the economic man of classical theory is not a man who has no end but the making of money. He is not a man who is concerned only with providing for his own consumption. He is simply a man who *in his capacity as*

---

[1] I have dealt with this problem at some length in my *Nature and Significance of Economic Science*, 2nd ed., chaps. i and ii. But I did not deal there with the problem of giving some meaning to everyday phrases such as 'economic cause', 'economic factor', etc. What follows may therefore be regarded as a supplement to these chapters. The solution here offered is entirely consistent with the somewhat radical approach of the general methodology there presented.

[2] This conclusion has actually been suggested by Mr. Hawtrey. See above, chap. iv, sect. i.

producer is concerned with the maximization of general purchasing power. His productive activities are not ends in themselves. They are not immediately subservient to particular kinds of consumption. They are purely instrumental to the augmentation of his power to purchase in general. He may want money for purposes of pushpin or poetry, for egotistical or altruistic reasons. But *as producer* he has no mixed motives. His motive is purely economic.

Here surely we have a way of making precise the distinction for which we are looking. The causes of war are to be regarded as economic if the objective is purely instrumental to securing for some person or persons a greater command of resources in general — a greater power of choosing alternative types of real income. They are to be regarded as non-economic if the objective is not instrumental to anything further — if it is definitely an end in itself rather than means for a number of ends.

At first sight this may appear very remote and abstract. But it fits very well with everyday usage. In everyday speech, we should say that a war waged to spread the principles of a certain religion, a genuine crusade for instance, was due to non-economic causes. But the causes of a war that was waged to secure better openings for trade or freer access to certain raw materials (the so-called Opium Wars of the last century, for instance), we should certainly describe as economic. Both types of war involve economic problems in that both involve problems of the disposition of scarce means — scarce man power, scarce capital, scarce natural resources. Both types of war may be waged by men having a multiplicity of ultimate objectives. But, in the one case, the war is a means to a specific and ultimate end; in the other, it is merely instrumental to the achievement of ends in general. The characteristic of the economic motive is the lack of specificity of the means with which it is concerned.[1]

5 *The Rules of Historical Explanation*

Now in investigating the historical significance of economic causes in this sense, one rule must always be obligatory. In diagnosing the causes of any particular war (or war in a situation of a particular type), it is not enough to say that economic interests are involved; we must specify *whose* economic interests. In analysing the phenomena of social life, we must always remember that, although the individual is affected by his social environment, yet action in society is always the action of individuals; and it is always the conceptions by individuals of their own and other people's interests which are the subject of conscious action. In order that military action by the government of a national group may be said to be due to economic causes, it is not necessary that the economic interests of every member or a majority of the nation should be involved. It is indeed, as we have seen, not impossible that this should be so. But it is not necessary that it should be so. It is quite easy to think of cases where the interest is merely that of the absolute monarch or of a group of predatory financiers. If our diagnosis is to be adequate, it is essential that, at every stage, the connection between economic interest and the economic subjects who have the interest should be very clearly indicated.

At the same time, it is important also to show that the interests diagnosed are actually realized and operative.

---

[1] Following the same line of analysis, the distinction within the sphere of general strategy between military and economic objectives will be seen to be a distinction between objectives having more or less specific utility for the ends of particular operations. The destruction of a cargo of iron ore is an economic objective; the destruction of steel guns is military.

APPENDIX

To show that such and such a war was due to economic causes it is plainly insufficient to show that certain groups or classes benefited after the event. It is hardly possible to think of any war in history which has not brought some benefit to someone. But the benefited are not necessarily the responsible. Because sculptors and monumental masons did well out of the boom in war memorials after the Great War of 1914-18 we should not say that they bore any great responsibility for its outbreak. The receipts of the manufacturers of armaments and the owners of raw materials used in war are obviously raised by the outbreak of war, or at least by measures of warlike preparation. But it is a far cry from the recognition of this very obvious fact to the demonstration that wars are the result of the pressure of armament interests. To show that economic interests play a part in the causation of war, it is not enough to show that they benefit *ex-post*; it is necessary to show that it was thought that they would benefit *ex-ante*, and that this conviction was an operative factor in the actual framing of policy.

This is not a demonstration which can be undertaken by purely speculative methods. To establish the significance of economic causes we have to show their actual operation in practice. To understand the mode of working of any kind of cause, it is proper and useful to construct models, as it were, of typical situations, and to investigate how different motives may be *conceived* to operate. But to establish a logical possibility is far from establishing an historical influence or a present tendency. To do this it is necessary to show, not merely that the factors postulated in the model were actually present in certain circumstances; it is necessary also to show that they were the important and significant factors. A theory may be misleading, not merely because of logical inconsistency, but also because of inadequacy to the facts of the situation; and as we have seen, it is probable that some at least of the attempts which have been made to explain war in terms of economic causes have been deficient for just this reason. They are not logically impossible. But they do not fit the facts. It is not logically impossible, for instance, that all wars and dangers of war might be due to the machinations of the manufacturers of armaments. But reference to the facts seems to show that, while occasionally such measures may have been effective, it is a gross error of perspective to suggest that they have been proportionally very important. Only by continual testing of hypotheses by reference to historical fact can we hope to make progress in such inquiries.

When we refer to historical fact, however, we are likely almost always to be confronted by the difficulty that motivation is not simple. In the majority of cases where wars of any importance are involved, we find that more than one type of cause has been operative. We find that different groups with different types of motives have been influential. We find that even within one group, or within one individual consciousness a mixture of motives has been present. It is perhaps possible to discover pure cases. Few would argue, for instance, that the First Crusade was tainted by much economic motive or that the Fourth was inspired by very much else. But such cases are the exceptions. In most cases we find the desire for general wealth, lust for glory or revenge, devotion to duty or the dictates of particular religions, not to mention all sorts of cruder unconscious motives, all operating side by side. Considering the complexity of social action, it would be surprising if this were not so.

Recognition of this obvious fact does not, however, mean that inquiries concerning the action of particular causes are useless. For what we are out to do is, not to establish (or to refute) a uniform explanation of history, but to discover the rôle played by a particular type of cause in different types of situation. We want to discover, not whether or not economic causes are *exclusively* operative in the causation of war, but what is the significance of the part they play in different situations. We may not often find cases where the economic motive is exclusively operative. But we are content if we can find cases where it is predominant — or at least strongly co-operative with others. And although this is often a task of great difficulty, there is no reason to suppose that it is a task which cannot be undertaken. It involves indeed the kind of judgment upon which most decisions of everyday life regarding human relations are necessarily taken. We cannot attain quantitative precision here; for quantitative judgments in such a sphere are almost unthinkable. But there is no reason why, with due critical self-consciousness, we should not arrive at some sense of proportion.

6 *Social Structures as Causes*

There is yet another sense in which we may speak of economic causation.

Our inquiry has not been purely or even predominantly historical. It has not been limited to the explanation of particular incidents. The object has been to discover, not merely whether economic causes have operated in particular cases, but also whether there are any common characteristics of the different particular cases and whether there are typical situations in which they may be expected to recur. The ultimate aim has been not history but sociological generalization. Thus, for instance, we found that some wars were waged in the interests of particular groups of investors. But our inquiry did not rest there. We went on to inquire in what circumstances such groups would be politically influential, and whether there were broader features of the social and political situation, which accompanied such influence. And having found that there were such features, following an intelligible usage of everyday speech, we spoke of them too as causes.

It is just at this point that we need once again some precise means of distinguishing economic from other influences. Fortunately the same mode of approach that we found useful earlier, enables us to make the distinction which we need here. If the institutions whose existence is accompanied by the emergence of such tendencies are concerned with the organization of general power to satisfy a variety of ultimate needs, then we may describe them as economic; if they are concerned with the achievement of more specific ends then they fall under some other heading. Thus if, as Marxian communists have contended, the urge to certain types of war is ultimately associated with the institution of private property in the means of production, we should be entitled to describe it as economic in origin. Again if it were to be associated with certain forms of the institution of slavery, it would fall into the same category. If, on the other hand, it were to be associated with certain forms of political organization or the prevalence of certain religions, it would not come under this classification.

Now obviously here, as in the case of more restricted investigations, the influences may not be pure. There is in fact a strong probability that typical situations conducive to conflict may be the resultant of more than one general kind of influence. There is nothing which obliges us to assume that all social phenomena must be capable of being attributed to one kind of cause. And clearly even the influences which we take as ultimate may themselves have more than one aspect. Private property, for instance, may serve the economic purpose of organizing general productive power; but it may also be held in certain circumstances to derive its status from motives less instrumental in nature — desires for self-expression or the preservation of independence and so on. But this need not deter us. Here, as in the investigation of the motivation of particular actions, our concern is, not to establish an ultimate sociological monism, but to attempt to indicate the existence and the relative weight of influences which, on the level of inquiry which we chose, may be taken as ultimate data. In the final analysis nothing is assumed to be ultimate. It is merely a question at what point it is convenient to break off.

In the foregoing essay, the investigation was broken off at the point at which it was discovered that the existence of independent sovereign states, both directly and indirectly, gave rise to clashes of interest which were likely to lead to war. It was not denied that the existence of independent sovereign states was itself capable of further explanation. But it was felt that, since the main aim of the essay was to find causes susceptible of elimination, the discovery of this critical weakness in a political structure obviously capable of modification, was a point at which that aim might perhaps be said to have been sufficiently realized.